Trimingham's Brighton

Adam Trimingham

To Sue and Elly

Cover illustration by Gerald Lip

ISBN 0-9533493-2-2

British Library Cataloguing-in-Publication Data.
A catalogue record for this book is available from the British Library

Published by Pomegranate Press, Church Cottage, Westmeston, Sussex BN6 8RH

Acknowledgements: The publishers wish to thank the Evening Argus, Brighton, for permission to use photographs from the newspaper's archives

Printed by Ghyllprint Ltd, The Ghyll Print Centre, Heathfield, Sussex TN21 8AW (01435) 866211

Contents

The author today.

Wrong Way Orange Killed Him

*M*y long love affair with Brighton began in the summer of love, 1967, when I happened to spend a couple of weeks in the town on holiday. Like most visitors I knew the place only as a stunning but seedy place by the sea, reeking of stale chips, candy floss and spivs. I was delighted to find during this fortnight that it had all kinds of subtleties and surprises well worth exploring further.

The holiday was at the end of August. By the start of November, I was installed with my wife and young child in a Regency flat at Lansdowne Place in Hove and working for the *Brighton and Hove Herald*. For all this, we have to blame John Connor, the best journalist I have ever met and the greatest single influence on what I may laughingly refer to as my career.

I'd read the *Herald* on holiday and liked it, so I wrote off asking for a job. Connor, who was then the editor, replied and offered to meet me in my neck of the woods, Kensington, because he was attending an event at the Albert Hall. I didn't realise then how honoured I was because he seldom moved far from home. Typically neither of us had asked for any form of identification and as he was half an hour late for our rendezvous in a Lyons tea shop, I spent the time approaching several strange men asking if they were him.

Once we had met, Connor spent the entire interview telling me of the large amount of 'lineage' that could be made on the *Herald* by flogging stories to Southern Television, the Press Association and other papers for whom he was the Brighton correspondent. When, at the end of the interview, I diffidently asked about whether I had a chance of being employed, he replied: 'Of course. When can you start?'

I discovered that because of the low wages paid on provincial papers the *Herald* had become something of a journalistic dustbin. Many of the reporters had big disadvantages, but Connor was like a totter finding something good in all of them. Some of them drank too much. One chap was deaf (always a handicap in reporting) and another had only one arm. The paper was put to bed on Friday nights and Connor would let the copy pile up in huge bundles until

Wednesday morning. Then he would roll up his sleeves, sort out the rubies from the rubbish and set about producing a half decent paper.

Connor had been on the paper since 1941, joining on leaving school at 14. He rose to become editor 22 years later, and it wasn't his fault that the paper was in terminal decline by then. The *Herald*, like all other papers in towns where there was a provincial evening, was completely unable to compete with its rival for advertising. At the time it died the *Herald* was still selling a respectable 20,000 copies a day, but it was losing too much cash for anyone to keep it going.

I soon discovered that there was nothing Connor could not do journalistically. He had superb shorthand, excellent contacts and he wrote at speed. His knowledge of the town was encyclopaedic, and on the rare occasions when he had to use the library files which were numbered, he knew from memory where each one was. I thought him to be a mere newsman until, during an epidemic of flu, both the sports editor and theatre reviewer reported sick. On successive nights Connor produced a first rate report of an Albion home match and reviewed the latest production at the Theatre Royal, revealing a hitherto unsuspected thespian knowledge. Many hacks like to think of themselves as all-rounders, but few could match his abilities.

He was at his absolute best as a reporter. Always dressed in a dark blue striped suit, Connor was of indeterminate age and never changed noticeably during the 30-odd years that I knew him. To people whom he interviewed he appeared absolutely safe and, because his general knowledge was so great, he was soon able to converse in easy terms with them on whatever subject was at issue.

Connor's staff included a man called Allan Jenkins who liked drinking Double Diamond. It was his habit each day at lunchtime and in the evening to consume exactly eleven. When this task had been completed, he would abruptly leave the pub and go home. Quite why he had chosen this apparently arbitrary figure was not revealed, and although eleven DDs is a fair amount of drink, I never saw him the worse for it.

Chris Bale, the sports editor and an old Fleet Street hand, also enjoyed a jar. He told me that he liked to have sherry with scrambled eggs for breakfast, and before coming into work (he kept a gentleman's hours) he would often have a swift half in one of Brighton's many hostelries. Then, resplendent in his yellow waistcoat, he would set to work sub editing sports reports.

His pride and joy was a column, mainly of reminiscences, called Chris Bale's Corner. Typically, this would contain letters from elderly readers recalling the great teams of the past such as Arsenal's pre-war title-winning sides managed by Herbert Chapman. Together they would mention these fine players from long ago, almost invariably using their nicknames. A few journalists on the *Argus* who enjoyed Bale's columns sent in letters consisting entirely of bogus but barely plausible names and these were printed word for word.

A rare picture of my friend and mentor John Connor, for many years without doubt the best reporter in Brighton.

Jean Garratt, widow of a previous editor, could not type and had ferociously fixed opinions of a right-wing hue. It amused Connor, who enjoyed an argument, to discuss an issue with her (usually winning the day) and then later to employ her logic against some of the reporters who were generally more left-wing. But Jean's great gift was her tenacity. She would sniff out a story and would not let go, often forcing officials such as hospital administrators or borough engineers to give her information out of pure exasperation so that they would not be badgered any more. She looked like a sweet white-haired old lady, which in many respects she was, but her unsuspected terrier-like devotion to stories won her many scoops.

Dick Barton, the chief reporter, was a cheerful chap who looked like a teacher in a minor public school. He would breeze in, mark the diary, and not be seen again until tea time, by which time he'd been to Hove, which was his main beat, lubricated his throat with a few bevvies and written a few paragraphs. When asked anything about the paper, his twin responses were: 'Nothing to do with me' or 'Don't know a thing, old boy'.

Like Connor, Dick was devoted to lineage but for weekly rather than national papers. He spent many an evening covering dinners for the Sussex Association of this-and-that, most of which met in Brighton. The next day he would type away merrily with as many as nine bits of carbon paper in his typewriter as he wrote copy for all the weekly papers in the county.

'It may be only a penny a line for one, but it's ten pence a line for the lot,' he explained.

Shortly before he died in 1970, Dick did me a good turn. For many years he had written a column called Brighton and Hove Searchlight for the *West Sussex Gazette* in Arundel. The pay for this miscellany plus a few news paragraphs was a princely £6. 10s a week, more than a quarter of what I was paid on the *Herald*. I kept his commission on for twenty years, contributing over a million words to the *WSG* who, in turn, helped me through hard times financially until the powers that be decided they didn't want it any more. During its lifetime of sixty years the column had only four contributors: Conrad Volk, son of the man who started Volk's Railway, Jean Garratt's husband Tom, Dick and myself.

Dick's last command to me was: 'Remember, Trim old boy, they've got a colour coding system down in Arundel and you must write the column on yellow paper.' I scoured the stationery shops of Brighton for it, eventually finding some at great expense, and I wrote on it for months. Then a sub-editor phoned me up and said: 'Must you use that bilious colour? It makes our eyes ache! We often used to tell Dick about it but he insisted on using it.' Despite his foibles, Dick was a delight and when he died on Christmas Day that year, he was dearly missed.

The old *Herald* had preceded him by six months. It had been going since 1806 and its proudest moments had come in the early years when it had been the first paper in the country to report such triumphs as the Battle of Waterloo because sharp-nosed reporters of the time got the news from messengers giving details to the Prince Regent when he was at the Royal Pavilion. We were all made redundant and I decided to go to the *Argus*. The fine old headquarters in Pavilion Buildings closed, and we all had a sad farewell drink.

But the very next week, the paper was back on sale as if nothing had happened. A Worthing businessman bought the title for £50 and carried on printing it in Aldershot. After five months, Connor lured me back and returned to the familiar mixture of eccentricity, lineage and excitement. The paper lasted just 18 months, until the end of 1971, under three owners, none of whom succeeded in the impossible task of making it pay.

The Worthing man sold out to a trio of Brighton businessmen who altruistically wanted to preserve an independent paper. One was Harold Poster, owner of the Metropole, whom I never saw in the building. Another was Reg Elphick, boss of R. Green Properties, who understandably worried about the accounts. The third was an estate agent and councillor, Stanley Theobald, who could have had a golden opportunity to put forward Tory propaganda. To his credit, Stanley never interfered with a single word of editorial even though some of it must have pained him. But he got out wisely because he was not a newspaperman and Stanley's success, which was considerable, came because he had a matchless understanding of the things he did well. The three of them sold out to a maverick councillor called Michael Cohen.

After a few months Cohen called us all to a meeting and told us dramatically that he had reached a deal with new backers. Either he stayed and the paper would fold in a few weeks through mounting losses or he went and the paper survived. Having put this stark choice to the staff, he asked us to vote on it. Suspecting the truth, I proposed that we got rid of Cohen and this was carried. We later discovered that he had already sold it.

At this point, Connor decided to leave the *Herald*, which was a seismic event in Brighton journalism as he had been there man and boy. I said at the time that it was like a ship leaving a sinking rat. He bought the local freelance news agency and asked me to join him as his sole employee, which I did. The *Herald* employed as its last editor one Leonard Knowles, a ponderous and elderly alderman who was also a journalist. It was a lifetime's ambition for Len and he accepted the post gladly, but within two weeks the *Herald* was dead -for good this time - and, overcome with grief, Len died within the year.

I spent three happy years with Connor at the agency and together we covered some wonderful if sometimes disturbing stories, including the Maria Colwell inquiry and the collapse of the end of the Palace Pier when it was hit by a barge. I could never match his work rate, for he was on duty all the time. Connor lived and breathed journalism. It was the thrill of the chase that pleased him. Although he made a respectable living from it, his rate per hour must have been appalling and he never claimed half the expenses he was due because he simply wasn't that interested in the money.

We never discussed conditions of employment or expenses, and Connor paid me each week with notes from his wallet. We did not have a single argument or even a cross word. In the end I returned to the *Argus* when the staff negotiated a house agreement that gave them a 50 per cent rise in wages, and I could not expect Connor, who matched the Argus top rates, to do the same. We continued as friends until his death, and as the best possible tribute to him the agency he took over all those years ago is still known as Connor's because his name was so good.

Over at the *Argus*, things had been much the same since the war and they were to continue that way for a few years yet. The imposingly titled editor-in-chief was Victor Gorringe who had taken over the helm as a young man chiefly because most of the others were away at the war. When he started, the circulation was around 25,000, and by the time he retired in 1978 he had more than quadrupled it. There was some luck involved in simply being there when provincial evening newspapers were surging ahead, but Gorringe was a local man who knew what the readers wanted. By a happy accident, he became exactly like the typical *Argus* reader - a bolshie conservative with a fierce liking for the place.

In the editor's chair, and effectively the chief sub, was Barney Barnard, a cheerful, brisk man who put up headlines to match. Every time someone died a few weeks short of her 100th birthday he would have something like *Just Missed Her Century*. On an inquest report where someone had choked on a piece of fruit, he had *Wrong Way Orange Killed Him*. His famous and much anthologised one was *Man Found Dead in Cemetery*.

My own favourite was one he put up on a story of a man who collapsed at the wheel of his car while on a dual carriageway. As his lifeless form was being carried away to hospital, the scene was witnessed by his hapless wife who promptly had a heart attack in her car and keeled over dead. The man made a full recovery and Barney's headline was *No Need for Wife to Have Died*.

Old hands recalled the case in the 1950s when the jury was out on a case involving Lord Montagu and alleged homosexual activities. The headline was *Montagu: One Way or the Other*.

His deputy was a taciturn but highly effective man called Harry Cawkell, universally known as Mac. He did not suffer fools gladly, but to see him sub was an education. Rather fittingly he ended his career as he had started it, writing. He and I completed the *Argus* centenary supplement in 1980 together. Mac, who was a keen bird watcher, said at his farewell that he would never come back but would devote himself to watching wildlife at a remote cottage on the Dungeness marshes. He did and is there to his day, still contributing excellent Nature Notes to the *Argus*.

As news editor there was another rather dour man known as Jock Miller. He did single-handedly and without any apparent effort duties which it later took several people to fulfil. Pernickety and patient, Jock was expert at finding mistakes, and if any found their way through into the paper he was the ideal man to head off any complainants. After hearing half an hour of his patient explanations, they had usually calmed down enough to accept a small apology or a letter of correction.

While the top brass serenely carried on seemingly for ever, there was a seething mass of change beneath them with reporters coming and going all the time. Because Brighton was within commuting distance of London, many of them graduated on to the nationals and continued to live by the sea. Perhaps the best known of them was Jack Tinker, the theatre critic, who was so prolific that when he wrote features they had to be under another name, Luke Leavis. Jack was eventually snapped up by the *Daily Mail* where he stayed for more than twenty years. He won a national reputation as a critic, but I don't think he ever wrote better than when he was on the *Argus*. There is a memorial plaque to him in St Nicholas churchyard, right in the middle of the Brighton he knew and adored.

The reporters were a varied lot. One, Rod Badams, was a committed Christian, and he once submitted an expenses claim for a minus amount because he had made some personal phone calls from work. Another chap was sent to a meeting of Hove Policy and Resources Committee and never came back, completely disappearing. He was reported as missing but nothing more was heard of him. Robert Shelton, worthy successor to Tinker as theatre critic, was an obese American famous both for having discovered the young Bob Dylan and, many years later, for rewriting a rather impenetrable biography of him. Although large and sweaty, Shelton had great success in his mission of pursuing young women, mainly because his conversation was so delightful - an object lesson to all seducers.

The old offices at North Road were just how you would imagine a newspaper to look. They were dirty, untidy, and full of paper and cigarettes which periodically caused conflagrations when the carelessly chain smoking Colin Adamson was about. The typewriters were chained to the desks in case they were stolen. Every square inch of the painted walls was covered with yellowing cuttings of mistakes and misprints. A continuously moving conveyor belt took the finished copy into the composing room, where the linotype machines produced a familiar and intoxicating smell of hot metal. Among the operators was Danny Watts, who eventually reached the Guinness Book of Records for his stay at the paper, When he retired aged 88, he'd been there 72 years.

Nothing fazed most of the staff on the *Argus*. At the time of the Yorkshire Ripper killings, then unsolved, Sue Taylor was sent down to see a man in the front office who claimed to know who had committed the crimes. He fished around importantly in a briefcase for some minutes before pulling out an ageing document of doubtful provenance. Reading from it portentously, he announced: 'It was a social worker - with a wooden leg.' At this, Sue made her excuses and left.

I was threatened many times, not least when I was covering court and people wanted no publicity. But in those days the *Argus* reported every criminal case in Brighton and there was no way of avoiding that. I also got into trouble when writing about the unlovely Milner and Kingswood Flats, suggesting that they'd been put next to the police station so that the coppers could keep an eye on the villains. This prompted a full-scale march on the *Argus* led by an ambitious Labour councillor called Dave Hill. I confronted them myself, but they were pacified only by Jock Miller, who in the end promised them a space equal to that taken by my offending article to say what a lovely bunch they were.

On another occasion I was sent to a circus at Sheepcote Valley where the enterprising proprietors were offering free bags of elephant manure for people's gardens. I was deputed to bring it back, and brought the bag into the office where it was ready to be photographed. Gorringe happened to pass by and, and wrinkling his nose at the alarming odour, asked: 'What's that?' 'Elephant dung, Mr Gorringe,' was the reply, and he went on his way, puffing on his pipe as if it were perfectly normal.

Later that day, I took the bag home in a rucksack on my bike, as I do not drive. There was a disaster in Old Shoreham Road as I reached the traffic lights with Fonthill Road. I had to brake suddenly and, inevitably, a large load fell on my head. I retrieved what I could and dumped the manure on my allotment where it was supposed to grow jumbo-sized tomatoes. Sadly it was far too acidic, and they all immediately died.

The worst reaction I ever had to any story was when I wrote in less than complimentary tones about dogs and the mess they made in the street, then far worse than it is now. I received more than 80 letters, all disagreeing violently with the points I had made, and scores of abusive phone calls. One man said: 'When you leave the office on your bike at about 5.30pm tonight I shall be waiting half way along North Road in a souped up Ford Cortina. I shall rush along and mash you up until you are strawberry jam in the road.' I left at 5.45.

Another caller rang on the hour, every hour at home for a whole week just doing heavy breathing. It went on all through the night. Whether it was man or Doberman I shall never know.

Before joining the *Argus* I had never spent more than three years in any job, preferring to move around frequently. But with the demise of the *Herald* there was almost nowhere else to go and, in any case, I got the scope to write what I wanted and express my own opinions - something the *Herald*, for all its eccentricities, had never allowed. So, when I rejoined the paper, much to my surprise I never left again, eventually becoming almost its oldest inhabitant and a still point in a changing world.

In other towns and other trades, 25 years can be considered almost a blip in time, but in Brighton it is an eternity. Looking around me, I see hardly any colleagues who were there at the start, and precious few figures in public life who have survived all that time. In fact I cannot think of one person in a leading rôle in the town back in 1974 who is still there today. Brighton has changed greatly in becoming more mobile, for up until that time there was the solidity and immobility that most provincial towns possessed. Alderman Dorothy Stringer, who gave her name to the High School in Brighton, may have been unusual in being a member of the education committee for more than 50 years and never missing a meeting, but she typified the long-lasting nature of local civic life.

During that time I have written at least 20 million words and had most of them published. It is a huge output and shows no signs of diminishing. People who think that all I do is labour over a column each week are sometimes surprised to find that I write more than a hundred stories during that time. One editor, David Williams, did a word count on me and found that I'd written about 15,000 words in a three-day period. He calculated that between February and the Spring Bank Holiday I'd written the equivalent in words of *War and Peace*, but he added hastily that it was hardly of the same literary quality.

What I relish about all that is how ephemeral it is. Scarcely a syllable will be remembered beyond the next day, except possibly by some libel lawyer. Journalism emphatically is for the moment and deserves to be forgotten. You are only as good as your last story and that may not have been brilliant, so I am content to remember the characters and the causes rather than the carefree way in which I slung stories together.

Rough Seas and Brown Fingers

*T*rim, old boy,' said Dick Barton when he had breezed into the *Brighton and Hove Herald* office one morning 'it's worth an awful lot if you can come into work on an open top bus.' And on nice days, from his home near Hove seafront, that's exactly what he did. I also met a man swimming backstroke in the sea one summer day soon after I'd arrived. 'Worth a thousand a year to live in Brighton and be able to do this,' he said at a time when I was only earning that in total. But I had to agree with the principle of what he said.

When I arrived in Brighton from the middle of London I could hardly swim the width of the local baths. But I loved the sea and have always lived as close as possible to it. There's something about the crashing of waves, the scraping of the shingle and the strong scent of seaweed that is almost irresistible. And as well as being by the seaside, I want to be in it.

Within a year I could swim tolerably well although never all that fast, and Phil Bird, one of my news editors at the *Argus*, eventually persuaded me to join Brighton Swimming Club. Looking at all these heavily muscled chaps on the beach, I imagined that you had to pass some formidable aquatic test to join, but nothing of the sort was needed. Instead I became part of a fine and eccentric institution which proudly boasts that it is the oldest swimming club in the country.

Founded in 1860, the club was quickly joined by many leading professionals including Captain Camp, a one-legged swimmer and lifeguard whose motto was 'I dare the waves a life to save.' The good captain was long dead by the time I joined, but there were still some imposing members, such as the splendidly named former Mayor Alderman Percy Friend Friend-James. Another member was Tom Garratt, editor of the *Herald* before John Connor and husband of the garrulous reporter Jean.

The club had an arch below the roadway leading down towards the Palace Pier from the foot of East Street. It was a large space full of old wet suits, damp swimming costumes and an impressive array of boards for surfing, which was becoming popular in Brighton. Most of the members were pretty ancient, but what they didn't know about swimming wasn't worth knowing. They could judge the temperature of the water to within a degree and they knew all about currents. Swimming with them, even far out to sea, you never felt in danger because, of course, you never were.

The prince of all the swimmers was Jim Wild, a pawnbroker from Lewes Road who came from a long-lived family. Once, when he was well over 60, I asked him where he was going to on his Wednesday afternoon off work. 'Why, to visit my parents at Seaford,' replied Jim: they were both hale and hearty and in their mid 90s.

Jim was never one to boast in any way about his achievements, but they were amazing. He celebrated his 80th birthday by swimming round the Palace Pier. Even more remarkably, he had achieved the same feat at the age of 75 on a New Year's Day when the water temperature was just seven degree Centigrade - so cold that most people would start to suffer from hypothermia after just a couple of minutes. When well over 80, Jim would also put out the markers for the Seven Sisters Marathon near Eastbourne. Once fairly recently I met him on a winter's day in Hanningtons after he had been ill, looking distinctly red eyed and a bit shaky. 'Are you OK?' I asked him anxiously. 'Fine thanks,' replied Jim. 'I've just been round the pier again.'

Plenty of people would say that they went into the sea every day, but few really managed it. One who did was my friend Terry Sinnott, who entered the sea each day in 1973, posing on New Year's Eve with a giant board reading 365. Remarkably Terry, another big, strong man, was never once put off by high winds or raging seas, and he went into the briny at the appointed time.

Inspired by this I decided to do the same myself. I did it throughout 1977 and then continued into 1978. That Christmas I was struck down with a severe chill which made me shiver but there was no way in which I was going to be deprived of my record. On December 28, draped in blankets, I made my way down to the sea after being in bed all day. I waded out into the water at low tide, watched by anxious members of my family, and did the swim even though we were in the middle of the coldest snap for years. I completed the year and had a January 1 swim for luck. But the following day, even though it was fine, I ducked out deliberately, otherwise going in for a daily dip would have become an awful obsession.

Every time it was cold, TV and radio crews came down to the swimming club to watch us or hear us entering the sea. It was OK walking barefoot through the snow to dive in but for some reason it was always agony coming back out. Even worse was having to stand there looking jolly afterwards while the crew slowly filmed us yet again. I gave up regular winter swimming after entering the water on the coldest day of the century in Brighton during January 1987. The air reading was just 19 degrees F and the sea was 33. I decided that these were unlikely to be beaten and today I usually pack up in November, with just a festive dip on Christmas Day.

My real love is swimming in rough seas, although I am considerably less brave now than I once was. You can always get into a big sea, but it can be hard getting out because of the undertow. My nastiest moment came during a January gale with a south east wind blowing which made the waves break awkwardly. Terry and another swimming club member called Norman Swaysland got out safely, but I was caught amid a succession of huge breakers. Rapidly losing strength through the cold, I

Taking a dip in the sea off Hove. Although the sun is shining, it's March and the water is a chilly 47 degrees F.

17

began to wonder if I would make it before a mighty wave smashed me on to the pebbles, and I used all my remaining energy to claw my way up the shingle.

On another occasion I recall being in a sea so big that I was lifted well above the East Street groyne and I could see down the road itself. I nipped out of that one, but I wouldn't be so bold today. The club had a series of sea races each summer and I took part in them although being slow and awkward. I came last in the lot, whether it was a 200-metres dash from the pier to the East Street groyne or a mile-long trek round a buoy. My big chance came in the round-the-pier handicap, for which Jim Wild gave me a generous start, but I still managed to misjudge the current while everyone else did not and finished well behind the field. In desperation I arranged my own race: 200 metres of Old English Backstroke. I failed to come last this time only by dint of the fact that one swimmer could not see where he was going with this oddest of strokes and went off at right angles to the rest of us. But it proved that I wasn't absolutely always the booby.

I also twice took part in the annual pier to pier race held each July in Brighton. It is really for proper swimmers and is always held against the current to sort out the men from the boys. (The boys usually win.) The first year I took part, the sea was strong and there was a force five wind blowing. After about half an hour I felt seasick and came ashore by myself about two thirds of the way along. But worse was to follow the following year when the race was held in a smoother sea but against a tougher than usual drift. It took me 35 minutes to pass the Metropole and by this time I was starting to go backwards, knowing that the winner would already be clambering up the landing stage steps on the Palace Pier ready to receive his trophy. So that I would not cause any more embarrassment, I signalled to one of the rescue boats to come and collect me. But so exhausted and clumsy was I as I clambered aboard that I upset the craft and tumbled with the unfortunate occupant back into the briny.

The next year I reported on the race from the safety of the pierhead and asked the winner what he thought of it. 'A nice little swim,' was his nonchalant reply after completing the course in a quarter of an hour. And he added: 'It's good preparation for next week, when I'm going to swim the Channel.'

There was a real beach life in those days. Many people until about the last 20 years used to take longer lunch breaks than they do now. Indeed many office workers went back to their homes in the suburbs and had full meals. I used the time down on the swimming club beach sunbathing and mucking about in the water with my friends. At weekends, whole families would gather there. The beach was like an enormous social gathering place with scores of people there on fine days. It was a very democratic spot with everyone much the same wearing just costumes no matter how different they were with clothes on the rest of the time. And if bores turned up, which they did occasionally, you could always avoid them by diving headlong into the sea.

The old swimming club was in a building made out of reinforced concrete and at high tide during storms waves would crash against it, making the whole arch rock and completely blacking the windows. This began to tell on the structure, and it became festooned inside with poles and struts to hold it together. In the end the arch was condemned and rightly so, for it could have collapsed on us all. The club was moved onto a smaller arch across the other side of the lower Prom, and the beach was replenished with stones. This had the unfortunate effect of taking the club away from the beach, even though it was only by a few yards, and of ending the reputation of this beach as being a beautiful sun trap even on the windiest days.

Gradually the older members died or moved away, and new ones failed to take their place. Today no one even goes in from the club in the lunch hour, other times being more convenient, and few sit and sunbathe on the beach, although winter dips are still popular. I don't even belong to the club any more, but the sea is still my favourite friend in Brighton.

I knew nothing about gardening when I moved to Brighton. Now I know next to nothing despite having had an allotment for all that time. The trouble is that I've got brown fingers, and a lot of what I touch dies. My beans are often has-beens and I constantly have to watch my peas and cucumbers.

In 1968 I took a plot on the allotment site in Hove behind my home in Elm Drive, solemnly signing a declaration that I might have to get off the site within a year when the new Hove Hospital was built. In the event it took 30 years, half a lifetime for many human beings but a mere flick of the eyelid for the National Health Service. The allotment I took was nearest to my house, but it had two disadvantages. One was that it lay behind another plot, so that the council could not come and rotavate it; the other was that it was an inconveniently long way from the nearest water supply.

I had some entertaining neighbours. One was a socialist school teacher at Moulescoomb who liked to right the world's wrongs by leaning on his garden fork and talking about them. White haired, he told me he'd been there 35 years, which sounded an enormous time as it dated back to before the war.

Now I'm getting on myself and have been doing it for almost as long as him. There was also a cheerful Ghanaian called Joe who had an unfeasibly large number of children. He started with no knowledge of English gardening at all, but quickly came to have one of the best plots in Hove. His family used the allotment as a garden, spending every fine day there in the summer, and it was a treat to see them enjoying themselves there. Joe, as the only black man living on the Knoll estate, took what was easily the best way of combating racial prejudice. He

There's a steady supply of flowers and veg on my plot in Hove, one of 450 on the Weald Avenue site.

was simply immensely cheerful and kind to everyone, even to those who were his enemies because of the colour of his skin. The result was that he converted half of them, while the other half would grudgingly say: 'I don't like blacks, but I like Joe.'

Some of the other allotmenteers were distinctly odd. One did nothing but chop up wood all day into rather small sticks. I think he must have been a retired lumberjack. Another had a proper room complete with stove in his shed and obviously used to live there on occasions, probably to get away from his wife. A man of 91 had been married three times and still managed a daily visit, eventually

arriving by taxi when his legs could not make it up the hill from Poets' Corner where he lived. A rather stern looking old boy was found dead one morning in the allotments with a seraphic smile on his face, having suddenly dropped dead in the early hours from a heart attack. There must be many worse ways to go.

What they early all had in common was extreme antiquity, and it seemed that as soon as they died other elderly men appeared to take their place. But slowly the appeal of allotments has dwindled, and I would say that there are half the numbers tilling the soil in Brighton and Hove today compared with those in the 1960s. There was one exception to this decline, and that occurred in 1973 when we had the first great oil crisis and faint stirring of ecological awareness: all of a sudden hundreds of trendies took to the soil.

The site in Elm Drive had been half used as allotments and half a farmer's field in which you had the incongruous sight each autumn of a combine harvester being seen among the 1930s semis. Now the farmer was given notice to quit, and young couples in corduroy parked their Citroens around the corner and set to work planting exotic vegetables.

The old men saw all too clearly what would happen. These people had even less idea than me of gardening, and considerably less energy. Soon weeds grew and enveloped their American land cress or vegetable spaghetti. Blackfly destroyed their beans because they would not use any pesticides, and mice devoured many of their seeds. The last straw came with the drought summer of 1976 which was trying enough even for the most dedicated allotmenteer. The trendies could not cope with the incessant hand watering that was needed. By the end of that year they had all gone and the allotments reverted to their former size.

There is something rather appealing about allotment culture. The old men spend scarcely any money, raising their own seeds and making sure that they have fresh veg all the year round. They build their huts mainly out of redundant advertising boards, elderly doors and cast off window frames. Allotment architecture is bizarre, with sheds looking as if they could hardly stand up (the 1987 hurricane proved the point, with hundreds of huts, including mine, as victims). But I have seen a skyscraper shed several storeys high and another with a tilt greater than the Leaning Tower of Pisa.

My favourite time in the allotments is early in the morning when, contrary to rumour, almost no one else is there. Here in this 30-acre space with more than 400 plots I am usually the only human, but I am not alone. Not far away are cats looking for field mice, and occasionally a squirrel hops among the scraggy trees. Best of all, the allotment fox will wander around, and sometimes he is so unafraid that he will come and investigate exactly what I am doing.

For all my failures, and they are manifold, I have some successes too, and there is nothing better than fresh veg straight from the allotment that you have grown yourself. I hope to carry on gardening until I am pushing up the daisies, preferably in my own plot - and there are usually enough there to ensure that this will happen.

Another passion of mine is running, and I aim to do this every day, often trotting up to the allotment on summer mornings and pounding the streets of Hove in the winter. I usually avoid the seafront because of the large dogs that are there in the morning, and I steer clear of parks for the same reason.

For many years I took part in races, ranging from a five-miler (from the Portslade Sports Centre to the Devil's

Chugging towards the finish of yet another race. By this time the winner would have been on his way home!

Dyke and back) to marathons. I completed the London Marathon three times but always found it crowded. Far better was the Seven Sisters Marathon, which I completed ten years in a row in conditions which ranged from snow and ice to one of the strongest gales of the decade and brilliant sunshine. I did half marathons by the score, but when even my modest times started to worsen, I decided not to bother with competitions any more. What I like best is testing conditions with ice, snow and hard hills, but I will willingly settle for dawn on a spring morning with blood red colours shooting all over wispy clouds.

Running is a great tonic and an integral part of my life, I cannot imagine not being able to do it, and a little bit of me will die if I am ever prevented from doing so. I spend most of my working life cooped up in offices or council chambers, and it is a huge relief to get far away from computers out into the fields or open countryside.

Ripper versus Rumpole

*F*ew of us go to the courts willingly, and our knowledge of them may be confined to TV dramas such as Rumpole of the Bailey and Kavanagh QC.

I have never appeared before magistrates or a judge for any offence - even riding a bike without lights - yet I have spent more time in court than many lawyers, and while there gained a working knowledge of the law that is potentially extremely useful. Not only have I learned enough points to be able to defend myself to some extent should the need ever arise, but I also know which solicitors and barristers I would choose to have on my side and which I would avoid at all costs. This is because I spent years covering the courts in Brighton and Hove as a reporter.

Courtroom scenes invariably feature bewigged barristers, but most mundane work is carried out before magistrates, and many of them are unpaid amateurs. These days they are given a lot of training in how to administer the law and more particularly how not to draw attention to themselves, but no such restrictions applied when I first started covering Brighton court, one of the busiest in the south east, more than 30 years ago.

The magistrates who chaired the main courts regarded themselves as important characters in the town, and in a way they were. Some achieved national notoriety, such as the one who described mods and rockers convicted after Bank Holiday riots in the 1960s as 'sawdust Caesars'. No one really knew what it meant, but the phrase stuck.

I knew on which days I would prefer *not* to appear should I be hauled before the law. Those were Mondays, Tuesdays and Fridays when the courts were chaired by the two Herberts, Cushnie and Ripper. These fierce old gentlemen were averse to granting bail and liked sending people to prison. By contrast, genial Harold King, managing director of the *Brighton and Hove Herald*, never sent anyone directly to jail on any of the many Wednesdays when I heard him preside, while Dot Voller, the Fabian who sat on Thursdays, was a model of fairness.

Ripper presided over one case which attracted attention all over the country, not too long after Lady Chatterley's Lover had been allowed to be published following a celebrated obscenity trial in London. A Canadian bookseller in what is now the North Laine area of Brighton was accused of stocking obscene books. His name was Bill Butler, and he was a genuine literary figure rather than a porn merchant. For some arcane reason the case could not go before a jury and instead went before the worst possible magistrate, Herbert Ripper.

Even though Butler was defended by John Mortimer, writer of Rumpole, and the defence brought forward a host of eminent witnesses, there was no way in which Ripper was ever going to find the books other than filth. The case was lost and Butler was convicted, to the general dismay of almost everyone connected with it. Ripper had the last laugh, for the *Evening Argus* unwisely used a picture of graffiti that appeared all over the town announcing that Ripper was obscene. The wily old JP successfully threatened the paper with libel proceedings and was paid a considerable sum in compensation which he donated to the poor box.

The man with all the legal brains at the court was a fat scout-master from Worthing called Albert Tritschler, clerk to the court. Tritschler knew his law and was seldom worsted by anyone. He regarded the magistrates with a somewhat proprietorial air, so much so that in one case, where a rather snotty barrister was appearing for the defence, he announced: 'My magistrates will now retire to consider the evidence.' The barrister retorted quite correctly: 'They are not *your* magistrates, Mr Tritschler. They are *our* magistrates.'

The courts in Edward Street were then new and riddled with design faults. One was that no one could see the magistrates from the front rows, so for years these were never used. Another, more serious, error was that there was an unprotected area from the entrance to the court from the cells and the dock. Prisoners got to know of this and would periodically make a run for it, often getting away. But a quick-witted regular once thwarted an escape attempt. Agnes Eckert, who was 78, came to the court for live entertainment and claimed it was better than the cinema. She quickly jammed her walking stick between the handles of the main court door, and the prisoner was captured immediately.

There were quarter sessions held at Brighton conducted by Charles Doughty, QC, whose father, Sir Charles had held the post before him. Doughty was a red-faced, permanently choleric man who regarded most defendants as scum, retaining a particular dislike for Irishmen and people who had once served in the Guards. What inspired these prejudices no one knew, for Doughty was not given either to introspection or to interview, but woebetide anyone called Paddy and wearing the wrong tie.

For most of his long career in Brighton, Doughty sat in the old law courts at Brighton Town Hall where the acoustics were so bad that after he had muttered his improbably long sentences reporters had to go over to the shorthand writer and ask what he had said. He was so hard on criminals it was rumoured that a permanent judge was kept on appeal to reverse the sentences. I once saw him send a man to jail for seven years for stealing a pork pie. The punishment was reduced on appeal to probation.

Doughty was disliked by almost everyone connected with the courts, but one old lag got his own back on him in an effective manner. Breaking into the law courts (which was almost as easy to do as breaking out), he got into the Recorder's room, found his wig and boiled it hard in an electric kettle. It was reduced to about a quarter of its size and was of no use any more, which doubtless consoled the villain as he was despatched to a few months in prison by one of the Herberts next day.

I never thought that Doughty had a sense of humour until his last day, when the usual hypocritical tributes were paid to him from the barristers and solicitors all the way down to the probation officers and the press. In his speech of response Doughty announced that he happened to have received a card that day from Parkhurst Prison signed by one of the many people he had despatched there. It read simply: 'Having a wonderful time. Wish you were here.'

He was also Conservative MP for East Surrey, a seat latterly inhabited by another and much more famous barrister, Sir Geoffrey Howe. I find it impossible to imagine him dealing with constituents other than sentencing them to long periods in clink: perhaps he simply ignored them. But now that there is so much political correctness in courts I sometimes have a sneaking regard for Doughty and his form of instant, red-necked, scarlet-faced justice.

Over in the coroner's court, held in the basement where, appropriately, there was a freezing cold air conditioning system, there was another dynasty run by the Webb family. Ronald, coroner for most of the time I covered inquests, had succeeded his father in the post, and his son Roderick probably could have continued the tradition if he had wished to do so.

Unlike the Recorder of Brighton, the Coroner was a kindly man, but he had a habit of taking everything down laboriously in longhand, repeating statements as he did so. This occasionally led to unintentional humour which made me rush out of court, clutching a hankie to my face to prevent the distressed relatives from seeing my merriment.

Once he was conducting an inquest on a man who fell into a basement and died. The medical evidence revealed that he had suffered from every complaint known to man - cancer, heart trouble diabetes, gout, arthritis, Parkinson's disease, the lot. It was a wonder he was still alive before the fall, let alone afterwards. Webb took a full five minutes to write down this depressing catalogue of frailty. Then, whipping off his glasses with unexpected animation, he turned to the witness and said: 'Do you suppose, in your opinion, the deceased could have LEAPT to his death?' I did not give myself time to hear the reply.

Ronald Webb was responsible for an interesting change in the conducting of inquests. For years coroners recorded verdicts on the balance of probabilities rather than having to possess conclusive proof, as in a criminal trial. In cases where people had been depressed and had gassed themselves or taken an overdose, the likely verdict would be suicide. This was precisely the verdict which Webb recorded on a young man who fell to his death over the cliffs at Roedean.

But the youth's father, a stubborn tax inspector from Belfast, had other ideas. He challenged the verdict in the High Court and won a rehearing of the inquest at which Webb could do little but record a verdict of accidental death even though it seemed strange that the lad had climbed a fence at the edge of the cliffs before falling. All coroners, especially Webb, were much more cautious about suicide verdicts after that, and when you see the official figures about suicide, you can safely double them because of it.

Courts are sombre places where usually you see the worst side of human nature. But there could be moments of light relief, too. One came in a case where two people on a tandem were accused of careless cycling and convicted after a minor crash in the London Road near Patcham. The man on the back appealed on the grounds that he had not been in charge of the bike at the time. Yes you were, said the Crown, because you were pushing. No I wasn't, said the cyclist, because we were making a right turn and the chap in front was in charge of the steering. Deservedly he won his case.

It was a pleasure to watch the best solicitors do their stuff. Howard Johnson, the former MP for Kemp Town, would perform dazzling histrionics in efforts to get bail for the villains he was representing before their cases were sent to the Quarter Sessions. The silky skills of Cyril Chapman beguiled many a magistrate (although not often the Herberts) into exercising clemency for his clients. David Laing, my personal favourite, was so patently sincere that he secured acquittals in the most unlikely cases.

At the other end of the scale was a porcine barrister who once spent twenty minutes before Herbert Cushnie delivering the most dire speech of mitigation for someone accused of careless driving. Cushnie turned to his fellow beaks and said in a stage whisper: 'How much longer do we have to listen to this tosh?' The barrister stopped momentarily and continued for another ten minutes. The accused received a heavier fine than might otherwise have been the case.

You didn't have to tell Howard Johnson how to make a case newsworthy. He and many of his colleagues knew how to produce a turn of phase that would appeal to the headline writers. But it sometimes took a little bit of persuasion from the press to liven up the presentation by the police inspectors who prosecuted in those days.

Best of the bunch was a chap called Norman Bolton who was not averse to our suggesting a few lines when we met before court in the canteen. Once he had two lads up who'd pinched a boat and sailed it round the West Pier in highly incompetent fashion. I said that he should put in the sentence: 'They were the worst sailors who ever put to sea.' He duly did so, and the case got into every paper next morning: without that phrase it would probably have made barely half of them.

And there would be humanity in the court, too. Desmond Barker, a giant but gentle West Indian, was a regular before the courts because he was always getting drunk. He'd be sent down for a few days, go back on the streets, drink too much and appear before the magistrates again. When this way of life led to a premature death, Barker naturally had no cash and would have had a pauper's funeral. But the court staff clubbed together to ensure that he got a decent burial and attended the service, too.

Vicious Cycle

I have been cycling ever since I was knee high to an Elswick-Hopper. The first time I was on two wheels was at the age of four when I lived in Canada, and on returning to London two years later I was allowed to ride all over the streets of the capital without supervision, amazing as it may seem now. So coming down to Brighton posed no particular terrors for me on two wheels, despite its obvious disadvantages of strong winds, huge hills and narrow streets.

I ride my bike daily to work and almost nothing will stop me. Even on the day of the 1987 hurricane I rode in as usual, dodging the beach huts and broken glass, although I got a puncture as a reward for my pains. Sometimes I go to work on days so wet that everyone else seems to be in cars and even the rain is driving. I will venture out in snow, which is usually quite pleasant for riding on, and ice, which is less so. Fog can be a problem, but my least favourite weather for cycling is a thunderstorm, even if the chance of being struck by lightning in urban streets is small.

Although I occasionally sortie out into the country, most of my riding is achieved in town, and I cover about 3,000 miles a year. That may seem a lot but it's small compared with some cyclists. One sub editor on the *Argus* cycles daily from Lancing to Hollingbury and some years ago we had another who cycled into Brighton from Bognor until, sadly, he was struck by a car near the King Alfred Leisure Centre in Hove and was never able to ride a bike again.

Bikes do not fit easily into the road pattern of Brighton. They appear to be more or less invisible to a substantial minority of motorists and yet they seem threatening to pedestrians, especially when ridden by kamikaze teenagers. The answer appears to be bike lanes, and the one along the seafront has been a huge boon to me even though its route leaves much to be desired. There is an embryo network of lanes elsewhere in Brighton, and eventually they should link up with each other. Every time I feel frustrated by this lack of progress I have to remember that only a decade ago there were no lanes at all in the town.

A cyclist's view of Brighton's roads is completely different from that of a motorist. You get to know the back doubles, such as the quiet roads over and under the railway lines rather than the busy ones. Nipping through the old cattle arches at Tamworth Road, Hove and Vale Road, Portslade is much better than waiting for the Portslade level crossing or cycling up Sackville Road.

You come to know the hills well. Many are long and cruel. Perhaps the worst is Elm Grove, three quarters of a mile long and seemingly steeper as you reach the summit. Bear Road and Wilson Avenue are gruelling, too, and I never like Mill Road at Westdene much. There are steep climbs at Albion Hill and Southover Street in the Hanover area of town, but the prize for the steepest hill of all is The Drove at Preston. I haven't seen many hills as steep as the top of that, even when going round mountainous regions of Europe.

The most dangerous road for cycling is probably the bypass, especially when you are going past the exits. Old Shoreham Road and the seafront run it close. The most dangerous junction is the Vogue Gyratory by Sainsbury's in Lewes Road. The most dangerous hill to descend is King George VI Avenue in Hove because the camber goes the wrong way. The most frustrating wait at traffic lights is where Portland Road meets Sackville Road in Hove.

At the start of the seafront cycle lane at Hove Lagoon. I've cycled daily to work in Brighton for more than 30 years.

I used to get angry with motorists who cut me up and tried to run me over, and I would sometimes try to gain revenge. Catching up the cars at traffic lights and delivering them a satisfying whack on the bonnet used to happen perhaps once a month. On more than one occasion I was chased by the enraged motorist afterwards, one even mounting the pavement in an attempt to ram me. In a comic interlude near Seven Dials, a driver tried to get out of his Mini several times to thump me but every time he tried to open the door I shut it again. Another one rolled down his window and spat in my face. I am afraid to relate that I returned the insult. It was a vicious cycle.

Perhaps drivers are becoming slightly better, but I have less trouble with them these days and my methods of dealing with them have changed. If they cut me up I try to get in front in a narrow stretch of road and then ride very slowly, weaving slightly so that they cannot overtake for a while. Eventually I let them go by, delivering a modest smile. If they are male and aggressive (as most of them are) and mouth insults I generally blow them kisses, which often brings on further paroxyms of rage.

What cyclists have to do is to be noticed. I usually wear bright clothing when riding my bike, especially at night. I give extremely pronounced hand signals and I ride about two feet out from the kerb in case anyone tries to push me into it. Riding on Brighton's crowded roads is a matter of survival, and I intend to carry on cycling.

But I musn't give the impression that cycling is a deadly battle of attrition against mean-minded motorists. A lot of the time it is still a joy. Bowling along the seafront, pushed by a south west gale, you can come close to breaking the speed limit. Riding on the cycle lane after a sharp frost makes a satisfying crackling sound. You can see things as a cyclist that you would never notice otherwise, and you can park almost anywhere. It's the most efficient method of propelling yourself along the streets and it's remarkably cheap.

Bikes are also the fastest way of getting around central Brighton. Each year Bricycles, the local cycling campaign, used to organise a commuter challenge, putting a bike against a motor bike, a car, a bus, a train and other, odder forms of transport. Invariably the cyclist won. When I have a speedometer on my bike I have got up to some good speeds on the flat, and the fastest I have ever gone on a bike is more than 60mph down a decent hill.

But they are not so fast over longer distances, as I once found to my cost. I was on duty one Sunday for John Connor when the *Mirror* wanted me to call on a home in Bolney. I don't drive and public transport is negible out there, so I hopped on my bike - only to find an hour and a half later that the bloke was not in. Told that he might be in Lower Beeding, I pedalled over there and found again that he was out. Total miles ridden: 50. Total time taken: four hours. Total copy written: none.

On another occasion, I had to interview Lord Chelwood, the former Sir Tufton Beamish, at his home at Blackboys twenty miles from Brighton. It was a filthy wet day, and I had to change under a hedge near his mansion before arriving so as to look half presentable. Oddly enough, although I did not draw up in his driveway as most people did, he never asked me how I got there. I was rewarded for my pains by seeing the skies clearing, and admiring the view to the coast. The Cuckmere River rose in his garden, and he could see all the way to its estuary.

I also gave a start to the High Sheriff of West Sussex, who inhabited a cottage under Chanctonbury Ring, by arriving silently on my bike. He was so accustomed to motorist giving him advance warning of their arrival by crunching along the drive that he almost had a heart attack when I shimmied silently up to the front door.

Bikes are not all that good for arriving at smart dos. Suits tend to wear out at the seat and become shiny. Trousers have a nasty habit of getting entangled in chains. Rain falls harder on cyclists than on anyone else, and riding bikes in the summer can be hot work.

For many years I have had a tandem. With my wife on the back, we once completed the London to Brighton bike ride, covering 66 miles in all, and she had never previously cycled more than twenty. One of the chief advantages of riding them is that they can take away the difference between strong and weak cyclists. They are also handy for carrying children, even if they cannot reach the pedals.

My wife and I tend to use it when going to dinner parties or receptions provided that the weather is not too awful, in which case she refuses. The advantage is that after we've had one for the road we can creep along the gutters on our way home, being no danger to anyone except possibly ourselves. You can't be breathalysed on a tandem, although you can be drunk in charge, and in practice policemen tend not to stop you unless you fall off.

Tandems are inclined to be noticed even in traffic, and often when I am riding one I get calls of 'Daisy, Daisy' or references to some long-gone commercial on TV which featured a bicycle made for two. They are regarded indulgently and far more fondly then ordinary bikes by most people, perhaps because of their rather eccentric appearance.

I also have a trailer which has proved remarkably useful over the years - ever since its disastrous first appearance on a camping holiday. The wheels kept falling off and there seemed to be no way of keeping the axles on. In the end, I wrapped the axle in the tent bag and rammed it hard into a socket hoping that it would survive the next few miles to a bike shop. That was in 1965 and it is still there today.

The trailer is useful for bringing back large amounts of shopping from Sainsbury's. I have taken a double bed on it and a wardrobe. When I had a lodger, I moved all his possession from Wish Road to Springfield Road on the trailer, which had a small mountain on the back. We got all the way there until it toppled because of the steep slope right outside his new house, but by then it didn't really matter. The heaviest thing I have ever carried on it was an old storage radiator which I took to the Leighton Road tip. It weighed 420 lbs, and it was a tribute to the trailer that it made the journey there.

I also still have the bike, almost full sized, which I rode in London when I was six. It is a 1934 second-hand Hercules and, although it is far too small for me now, I keep it out of sentiment. Once a year I oil it up, pump up the tyres and give it a spin along the seafront for old time's sake. It is one of my oldest and most treasured possessions.

One of the downsides of cycling is theft. I have had eight bikes stolen so far, and more will undoubtedly follow no matter how careful I am at locking them up. Even my deterrent of keeping bikes as scruffy as possible and riding them with cardboard boxes on the back failed when one was stolen from right outside my office in Dyke Road. Some thieves are opportunists, simply wanting a bike to ride home on, but professionals load them into vans. Curiously I have never read a case of one of these vans being stopped and the thieves arrested, but I suppose it must happen sometimes.

Biking will only become an unalloyed pleasure here if cyclists become the majority road users as they are in parts of the Netherlands.

Bearing in mind Brighton's geography and climate, I doubt it if will ever happen, but it's nice to dream.

Nearly home: the Brighton and Hove seafront cycle lane will eventually become part of a national network.

A Girl Named Maria

Most days as a reporter not much happens, especially when there are staff shortages and you are increasingly asked to provide more and more copy. You tend to stay in the office, shout down phones at people and turn dull faxes into something a little less turgid. But once in a while something really big happens and the adrenaline starts moving. Every decade or so there is a story so big that you tremble with excitement.

When the IRA bombed the Grand Hotel in 1984 we asked ourselves afterwards whether there had ever been a bigger story in Brighton. We thought of the time when the town was sacked by the French in the sixteenth century, but then it was really only a small fishing community. We thought of the second world war, but that applied to everywhere. The bomb was really the most sensational tale I have ever covered, and of course I did not do it alone.

I'd been at the Grand until less than two hours before the bomb went off, drinking in the bar with colleagues until 1am having completed the last of my daily diaries for the paper. I did not hear the blast even though I live less than two miles from the hotel, but no sooner had I gone to bed then I was awakened by the insistent noise of the telephone. It was Frank Hayward, a timekeeper at the paper, and incidentally a stalwart Labour member of Lewes District Council. 'There's a big bomb alert at the Grand,' he said. My wife, who was working for *Southern Sound* at the time, said: 'Don't bother about it - it's only old Frank.' But I had to check it out and, sure enough, something was wrong.

I dashed down to the Grand. The irony was that I, without a police pass, could not get through the security cordon, while national newspaper reporters staying at the posh hotels were already there. I got into the Brighton Centre, which was not much use, and instead made my way to the office, where my job was to wake up every other reporter on the paper. This I managed with one exception, and by four in the morning the newsroom was as busy as it had been on a normal day at noon. (The reporter I'd failed to wake up sauntered in at nine as usual and said: 'Is anything happening?')

I returned to the conference centre at about that time when Mrs Thatcher, despite the deaths and her own narrow escape, had decreed that it should be business as usual. There was a strange and subdued atmosphere, with the people at the Grand wearing temporary clothing they'd borrowed from the Western Road Marks and Spencer, and with security amazingly tight but seven hours too late. It was an impressive example of the British stiff upper lip, but it was an ordeal for all concerned and we were thankful when it was all over.

The *Argus* sold something like 180,000 copies that day, a record which has held ever since. But the bombing, apart from wrecking the lives of many families, also changed irrevocably the face of seaside conferences. Gone for ever were the carefree days when people could just walk into the bars of any big hotel and hobnob with cabinet ministers, or when Harold Wilson could walk apparently unescorted along the seafront. Instead the strict security cloak was imposed.

Murders have not been uncommon in Brighton, so the case of William Kepple, accused on January 6, 1973, of killing a seven-year-old child did not cause much of a stir in the national press at the time It was headlines in the *Argus* but the murder seemed to be a typical sordid, domestic affair.

How wrong we all were. It proved to be the most sensational case of 1973, probably the best news year of the century in Brighton, and the reverberations are still being felt to this day. For immediately Kepple had been remanded in custody charged with murdering Maria Colwell the real story started to emerge,

Nothing could be published until after the trial of Kepple, which was set for May. He was duly sentenced to seven years in prison on a manslaughter charge which was no less than he deserved and which many felt was lenient. As he was an Irishman (although not in the Guards) he would have undoubtedly have received a far harsher sentence had Charles Doughty been presiding at Lewes Crown Court at the time.

The story of a seven-year old child being beaten to death and then wheeled in her pram from the Whitehawk estate to the Royal

The IRA bombing of the Grand Hotel in 1984 was the most sensational story I have ever covered.

Sussex County Hospital was shocking enough, but what was far worse was that nearly everyone in Maresfield Road had known about it. They had repeatedly warned the authorities that Maria had been ill-treated, and yet nothing had seemingly been done.

Then it emerged that Maria had been put in care like every one of her mother's 15 other children. She had been placed in the loving care of a couple called Cooper who lived in Ditchling Road. But when her mother hitched up with the violent and unpredictable Kepple, she successfully applied to have the child returned to her.

Stories abounded of the terrible treatment Maria had received; how she had been made to perform tasks like a drudge and singled out for ill treatment. She was little more than skin and bone when she died, and was about half the weight of a typical seven year old. Her school picture, showing a sweet, dark-haired little girl, served to enrage the kind hearts of Brighton whenever they saw it.

The man who realised right from the word go what was happening in Whitehawk was local Tory councillor Danny Sheldon, a man of genuine passion and tremendous intuition. He managed to persuade two other men of influence, Andrew Bowden, MP for Kemp Town, and Victor Gorringe, Editor of the *Evening Argus*, that something should be done.

A huge petition demanding action was collected, and East Sussex County Council, which had just taken over responsibility for social services from Brighton, decided to hold a private inquiry into what had gone wrong. But this was not enough for Danny Sheldon, Whitehawk, or most of Brighton.

By this time the noise and stench from Brighton had reached the ears and nose of Sir Keith Joseph, Secretary of State for Social Services. He ordered a full inquiry, to be held in public, and to be fully independent. It sat for the whole of the autumn and it was amazing. There has never been anything like it before or since.

Everyone involved in it was a character, ranging from Thomas Field-Fisher, QC, the charismatic chairman who had a flair for publicity, to Bill Sansom, the charming copper who guarded the door to the drab upstairs room in Western Road where the daily drama took place. The nature of the case and their involvement made the story one of local and national significance. Every day, crowds of people turned up to hear the evidence, and the case was headline news in all the national newspapers for the whole of the autumn. Meanwhile the *Evening Argus* reported every single word. It's probably no coincidence that this era coincided with what was the highest ever circulation of the paper, around 114,000 copies a day.

The public was baying for blood, but the question was whose it would be. The awful Kepples were too obvious and, in any case, one of them was in prison and the other never attended a single session. Many neighbours wanted officialdom to be on the rack but when you saw the people involved they were decent, involved and dedicated. The social worker, Diana Lees, Daphne Kirby from the NSPCC and Maria's teacher, Ann Turner, had all known something was wrong and they had all tried to do something about it. The problem was a fatal lack of liaison.

The inquiry lumbered to a halt around Christmas time, but not before an unexpected climax. Mrs Kepple's decision not to appear had been wise, but she still wanted to have her say. One morning when a quiet day had been expected and almost no other reporters were there, Mrs Kepple's barrister suddenly read out a statement from her. It gave her side of the story for the first time, and it was astonishing. In an instant, this crafty, flawed woman was seen to be a victim as much as a mother who allowed violence to be perpetrated on her daughter. She was in no state to have stopped her drunken husband battering Maria to death, but the two of them should never have been allowed to have custody of her.

I was working freelance at the time, and in all the years I sent stories to the national papers I never had such a wonderful show as I did the next morning. John Connor, my boss at the time, said that if he lived to be 300, which sadly he didn't, he would not experience such a superb period for news as 1973 was in general and the Maria Colwell case was in particular.

Maybe it seems wrong to mention her case in terms of finance. But I make no apologies for doing so. Had it not been for the Press, and the efforts of good men such as Danny Sheldon, it's unlikely that there ever would have been a public inquiry with the resultant changes in the law. I don't always defend what newspapers do, especially these days, but they behaved well in the case of Maria.

A good example of that came in one of those curious side issues that always arise in these big stories. A campaign was launched by a local estate agent called Robert Beaumont for people who murdered children to be executed. What we knew and most people didn't was that Beaumont had changed his name from Harvey Holford after being convicted a decade earlier of the sensational Blue Gardenia killings.

The question was whether Beaumont should be outed or not. We decided not to on the grounds that he had served his sentence and was now trying to rebuild his life. But we took a different line the following year when Beaumont stood for election in Kemp Town against Andrew Bowden on the same platform. We took the view that, as he was asking people to vote for him on this issue, Beaumont deserved to have his past declared to the electorate. The campaign flopped and no more was heard from him.

The inquiry duly reported. It resulted in the Children Act and many changes in the ways in which society protects young children. Every time a health visitor notices that your young child has bruising and questions are asked, however innocent the cause may be, this results from those sad events the best part of 30 years ago.

There was a lot of talk at the time by people saying that children should never be allowed to slip through the net of officialdom again. But of course they do, and the name of Maria Colwell is inevitably invoked on these occasions. Few children this century can have had such a profound effect on British society and even today when I see her sad, sweet face in her official school photograph, I feel a sense of helpless rage.

Another huge story was the great storm of October 1987. I'd gone home from a council meeting at about one in the morning. It was unusually warm and windy, but there was no hint of the tempest to follow. Living near the seafront, I felt the full force of the blast. An elderly neighbour took refuge in our house as his roof was partially stripped off, and we had to use torchlight and candles when the lights went.

It was too dangerous to venture out because of flying tiles and debris but the noise was colossal, much of it from the front where beach huts were being overturned. At dawn I went round the corner into Kingsway to see the family who cared for our baby during the day. One wall of their home had been partially demolished, and they were huddled behind a sofa in the front room.

At work, I went to the Royal Pavilion where a minaret had come crashing through the roof of the Music Room, then just restored after an arsonist had torched it in 1975. It was heartbreaking to see the mess, but eventually it was all restored once again. Even sadder was the destruction of all the trees, especially the giant elms in Valley Gardens. It proved a blessing in disguise at the Level, where a controversial council report had just been prepared suggesting the felling of some diseased specimens, and at St Peter's Church where the removal of elms opened up a splendid view of Sir Charles Barry's early masterpiece. But generally it was an awful day, and one minor ill-effect was that there were no autumn colours that year.

The paper did a splendid job and, amazingly, every member of staff made it into work despite all the problems. It might have achieved a record sale, beating the bomb editions, but for one factor: fallen trees meant that the vans could not reach most of the outlying areas.

I don't usually get involved personally in stories, but I did in the case of the Brighton bypass. Although I could see the advantages a bypass could bring, I was passionately opposed to the destruction of the Downs it would entail. As early as 1973 I had foreseen what form the opposition should take and had noted the need for an umbrella organisation to unite town and downs, and to make sure that everyone did not end up fighting each other.

As a reporter supposed to be impartial, I could not undertake this job myself, but luckily the right man for the job and one of my best friends, Peter Gavan, was at a loose end. Peter had been a colleague of mine at the *Argus* and was now working at Westminster as a lobby correspondent. He quickly accepted the need for action and so ABBA, the Anti Brighton Bypass Association, was born.

There was never much chance of winning the argument against the road at the inevitable public inquiry. Peter, a master plotter, perceived the need to drag out the proceedings as long as possible until a new government which was not Tory was elected. This was not through any anti-Conservative bias, but simply because a Labour or Lib-Lab regime would be less keen on new roads and would have fewer MPs in Sussex calling for them. In the event Peter managed to string out the battle so long that two general elections went by, but it was in the heyday of Thatcherism and the Tories won both of them.

The plotting was fascinating. Peter held monthly meetings in the front room of his home at Wish Road, a house I later bought from him when he moved to London and where I am now writing this story. Sitting there was a motley crew of councillors, amenity society organisers and ordinary people whose homes would be affected by the road. What was unusual was that Peter was the youngest there, yet such was the force of his argument that the meetings always accepted what he had done in their name and never quarreled over anything. What's more, they raised more than £20,000 in a few months to fight the inquiry. Peter also did sterling work in getting country lovers such the Society of Sussex Downsmen to come on board with cash and comfort. This was partly because, in Geoffrey Stallibrass, the Downsmen had a leader of equal intellectual agility.

Even the five-figure sum ABBA had raised was not enough to fight the big battalions on anything like equal terms. Every single official body bar Adur District Council was for the road. Most of them appeared at the inquiry with expensive barristers and expert witnesses. All ABBA could afford was a barrister and a traffic expert to cover a few days of the more tricky bits.

But Peter enlisted the support of John Tyme, the veteran anti motorway protester, who'd taken direct action in the past to stop roads being built. Sensing that this would not appeal to the mainly middle class bypass opponents in Brighton, Peter asked Tyme to tone down the protests in Sussex. This Tyme did so successfully that he was almost *too* polite. But he put the protesters' case effectively for the rest of the inquiry, and all he got was a fee of £25 a day plus his board and lodging at Wish Road.

The inquiry lasted from April until November in 1982. At 97 working days, it was then the longest that had ever been held into a road scheme that was not a motorway. But there was never any doubt about the result, and when it came a year later the road was approved in its entirety.

Interestingly, the climate changed considerably only a few years later when a second, shorter inquiry was held into the necessary compulsory purchase orders. Brighton Council, which owned nearly all the land, had changed political control and now resolutely opposed the downland dual carriageway. The inspector recommended that two tunnels should be built at Old Boat corner and Ditchling Road, and he questioned the need for the Hangleton link. But, scandalously, Government ministers intervened and squashed his very sensible suggestions. The road was built and is there today, a dreadful scar on the Downs.

But the battle was worth fighting. The delay of a decade gave many people peace for a little longer. The debate focused many people's minds on whether we really wanted a car-dominated society. ABBA was a model of how to fight a community-based campaign against officialdom. And, at a personal level, I made many lasting friendships from that campaign. Peter moved out of all our lives eventually to become a highly successful and well paid public relations consultant. To him it was little more than a mental exercise, but the quality of his leadership was appreciated by all those privileged to see it in action.

A few years earlier, I was involved in another campaign, this time to get rid of the old North Road baths and have a new pool built. In the mid-1970s, North Road, a gloomy Victorian building, was the only public swimming baths open in Brighton, while in neighbouring Hove the major pool at the King Alfred always shut down in the winter. I was a member of Brighton Swimming Club, and we fought extremely hard for the new pool to be built. There were endless delays, including the complete collapse of one scheme at the last moment in 1973. But at last the council raided its coffers, found some land and decided to build what is now the Prince Regent.

Our campaigning was still not over, however. The councillors in charge, who knew nothing about swimming, decreed that the pool should be only 25 metres long - smaller even than North Road and about the same size as the minor pool at the King Alfred. The swimming club tried hard to persuade the councillors that it would be too small, but to no avail. Undaunted, though feeling that the battle was lost, I arranged with friends for a protest to be held outside Brighton Town Hall before the fateful council meeting at which the final decision was to be taken. Particularly effective was the row of kids with toy baths and placards reading: 'Your new pool won't be much bigger than this.'

Unexpectedly we won the day. Before the debate even started Danny Sheldon, the councillor in charge of the project, announced that there would, after all, be a full-sized pool. The celebrations that night (although unfortunately I couldn't join in because I was covering the rest of the meeting) involved something stronger than chlorinated bath water.

The Prince Regent Swimming Pool in Brighton, built to the right size only after a long campaign by local swimmers. The Dome can be seen behind it.

The only other story with which I got personally involved was the fight to save the West Pier. When I came down here, the pier was fully open, but only just. It was a faded, fusty relic, clearly in danger of folding - and so it proved. In 1970 the southern end had to be closed because of its dangerous condition, and five years later the whole pier shut.

To me this was a tragedy. Here was the most beautiful pier in

Britain dying on its cast iron legs and no one was doing anything about it. Harold Poster, the big, brash owner of the pier who also had the Metropole and Bedford hotels within his domain, was piqued with the council for not allowing him to build a casino and other things on the pier that would have ruined it, so he refused to carry out any maintenance. The council felt that one decent pier was more than enough, and could not see the need to save it. I was outraged but, much more fortunately, so was John Lloyd, a wealthy but diffident shop owner in the Lanes.

When Lloyd heard that the council was prepared to accept the demolition of the southern end of the pier he decided to do something about it. He started the We Want the West Pier campaign and collect thousands of signatures on a petition. He also arranged a march on the town hall. The council, although it did not want to save the pier, had no wish to demolish it either, and acceded to Lloyd's request. In the meantime Poster, who'd done a lot for Brighton and liked people to know it, made an offer to the council: he would sell the pier to them for £1 and give them £250,000 towards the restoration, then a considerable sum. To Brighton's eternal shame, this offer was refused.

There was a long period of stalemate, and the pier eventually became the property of the Crown because no one else would have it. Hopes were raised three times during these years, only to be dashed again. First a young entrepreneur called Marc Turner offered to restore it, the disadvantage being that he had no cash. Then an ebullient tycoon called Alan Hawes, who'd already revived Rhyl in North Wales, came along with a scheme to build an enormous Ferris wheel on the end. By this time the council was so desperate that it was accepted, and Hawes strode proudly on to the pier to look at his trophy. He was a big man and the planking bowed under his tread, but fortunately he did not fall in. Unhappily he too failed to have the right amount of cash.

The best chance of all came when Merlin, a company with a proven track record of historical restoration, came along with ambitious plans - but once again, and most unexpectedly this time, it ran into trouble. The pier seemed doomed and even my old friend Councillor Smith, who had become chairman of the campaign, threw in the beach towel. But a retired schoolmaster called Bryan Spielman had other ideas, and he managed to keep the pier campaign group going just long enough to hand it over to more professional people, such as the present board of the Brighton West Pier Trust. With a combination of Lottery and private cash, I am convinced now that the pier will saved.

Sadly neither John Lloyd nor Bryan Spielman lived long enough to see the pier revived. But both were utterly convinced that it would be, and but for them it would never have happened. When eventually, some time in the Millennium, I step on to the gleaming, restored pier, I shall stroll into some bar or other on it and have a quiet drink in memory of them both.

There have been so many other big and enjoyable stories over the years. There was the row when Stanley Theobald, Tory to the core, suggested that the newly completed Brighton Centre should be offi-

Britain's only Grade One listed pier, the West Pier, still beautiful despite thirty years of neglect.

cially opened by Jim Callaghan, who was Labour. Theo won the day, as usual, by pointing out that Callaghan lived locally and did happen to hold the highest office in the land. What's more, he did a very nice job of it at the ceremony.

The biggest battles between Mods and Rockers occurred in the early 1960s, a few years before I came to Brighton, but I did witness the tail end of them, and highly unpleasant they were, too. There was a lot of stone throwing and deck chair burning on sundry Bank Holidays, with huge gangs of disaffected youths looking for trouble with each other in a slightly bored and menacing fashion. It all served to make me glad that I'd never had the temptation of joining either side - although I'd owned a scooter, I was too hairy to be a Mod and too soft to be a Rocker.

In one of the last outbreaks of violence the police had the brilliant idea of lining up the troublemakers and taking the laces out of their boots. Deprived of being able to kick their way into trouble, they left meekly. Whether as a result of this action or not, they never returned, and Bank Holidays have been largely peaceful since then.

One of the best rows in Brighton was twenty years ago over the proposal to establish a nudist beach in Kemp Town. Because it was the first one in a big town,and because Brighton has a risqué reputation, it caused huge interest all over the country. Chief protagonist against the beach was John Blackman, printing company boss, Tory councillor, ex-naval man and noted wit, who fulminated against it in perfectly formed quotes. For the beach was another Tory councillor, Eileen Jakes, a voluble publican noted for her tenacity and (for the tabloids) her readiness to do a Page Three pose on the shingle, even though she was twice the age of most regular models. The nudists won the battle of the beach, and it was screened by mounds of pebbles. The worst fears of its opponents have not come to pass, and most people don't even tknow that it's there.

Other stories? I remember when a barge nearly destroyed the Palace Pier. It happened in 1973 when the barge broke away from its moorings and started cutting into the pier head. Bit by bit, the pier began to collapse until, with awful creakings and groanings, a fair bit of the lovely old theatre toppled into the sea.

Although the wind died down and someone managed to get hold of the barge, the theatre never reopened after that incident.

Luckily the pier was revived and three years afterwards it was sold to the current owners, who have made a huge success of it. There was one odd incident in the sinking. Among the casualties was an old red phone box which used to be near the pierhead. A few weeks later divers went down to recover the coin box - only to find that someone had been along before them.

There were fires such as the one at the Madeira Hotel in Marine Parade, which killed seven people, and the blaze at the Music Room of the Pavilion started by a jilted lover. Brighton has had more than its share of blazes and almost every famous building in town was been alight at one time or other. The most spectacular blaze was that of Johnson's, an old department store in Western Road, which went up in flames one Guy Fawkes' night in the 1970s. And the best one I saw personally was at the Lewes Road Sawmills near the cemetery. In both those cases no one was hurt, and the fire was a big free spectacle for the people of Brighton.

Thanks to modern fire-fighting methods the number of spectacular blazes has sharply decreased in the last decade or so, but in November 1998 came the exception that proved the rule. The fire at the Royal Albion Hotel in Old Steine was the biggest in the town since the one at Johnson's. Crowds gathered as flames shout out of the roof, and the smoke could still be seen more than a day later. The blaze was so great that at first is appeared that little would be left of the fine listed building that had been there for 150 years. But the owners quickly decided to rebuild it. With luck and skilful architects it should be possible not only to restore this hotel, but even to improve it, as happened to the Grand.

Another big story was the *Athina B*, an old crate of a ship which ran aground near the Palace Pier in January 1980. It quickly became a tourist attraction as efforts were made to remove it from the shingle, although in reality it was an unlovely vessel. Eventually, on a day so foggy that hardly anyone could see a thing, the boat was refloated - only to be towed away for scrap. The ship's anchor, on the pavement with a commemorative plaque, recalls the incident still.

There was also the time when one of the Red Arrows crashed into the sea while performing an aerobatics display between the piers. The plane went in a fraction too low, clipped the mast of a yacht and was sent spinning. Thousands of people, including me, saw it just miss the Palace Pier and plunge into the water, only to be followed by the pilot who, having used his ejector seat and parachute, landed more gently. Once again no one was hurt and it was a good free show, but a lot of people had a narrow escape.

Most reporters enjoy covering these big stories, which are easy enough to write because they are so obvious. The real skill comes in making an ordinary little tale seem something special. That's when good hacks come into their own. If you are like Tom Moore, the talented and bibulous *Argus* reporter, and you can weave a magical tale while knowing only two of the 14 necessary facts, you are worth every penny of your meagre salary and the loyal readers will often appreciate that.

The magnificent Regency architecture of Brunswick Square in Hove.

They Came to Die, but Forgot

*A*lthough this book is about Brighton, I have lived in Hove during the whole of the 30 years that I've been here on the Sussex coast. This is partly because I regard Brighton and Hove as all one town and partly because I wanted to be near the sea. In the 1960s mortgage companies would not lend on old properties, so I had to go west to achieve my aim.

Hove managed to remain independent of Brighton for more than 100 years and regarded itself as a town of distinctive character. It certainly was, but by the time I arrived that character was moribund. The resort was elderly, crotchety and boring. It had its own institutions, but they creaked and the place was the poorer for it.

While Brighton had an orchestra at whose concerts a third of the audience came from Hove, the council would not even give a paltry sum of £200 each year towards the costs. It refused steadfastly to have anything bright and beautiful in the town, yet was only too happy to hang on to its bigger neighbour's coat tails.

You could tell when you were in Hove going along the seafront because not only did the coloured lights suddenly stop but the street lamps were also of a dimmer hue. If Hove was a cemetery with lights, as some suggested, they certainly were not on very brightly. A better gag was that people came to Hove to die and then forgot what they had come there for.

Hove was a surprisingly big town, with a population of 90,000 once it had swallowed little Portslade next door in 1974. It compared in population with Eastbourne, Hastings and Worthing but had far less character than any of those places because it was small geographically and therefore dwarfed by Brighton. It had a council, but one which was dire and dull.

The chief problem was a lack of democracy. Often, at elections which were held only every four years in contrast to the annual contests next door, half the councillors would be returned unopposed. Indeed, there were people who had been on there for twenty years or more without ever facing the electorate. Nearly all of them were Tories, and the one Labour man there for much of the time was indistinguishable from the rest of them. Despite this political uniformity, they were a rancorously bad tempered lot, always falling out with each other and often quitting the party to become ratepayers, or independents of some form. At one time the Ratepayers even had their own party which won seats. I always said that the Tories wanted to spend next to nothing and the Ratepayers wanted to reduce that still further.

It was highly appropriate that the council met in a museum since, when I first arrived, only one of them was under 50 and several were in their late eighties or even nineties. Senility was no bar to serving the electorate, and several councillors uttered not a single word at meetings. This at least had the merit of making them reasonably short, and while the council at Brighton often droned on for five hours, some meetings at Hove struggled to last fifteen minutes. It was the difference between active and passive boredom. Because the councillors were so ancient, they would die frequently, sometimes at meetings. One alderman actually expired while making a speech on the reorganisation of local government, possibly through its content. Instead of stopping the meeting out of respect, the councillors adjourned early for tea and then continued as before.

They met in the museum because the old town hall, a building of some distinction, had been destroyed by fire in 1966. The museum treasures were largely in store and, scandalously, the council decided to sell them - even those bequeathed to Hove by its own citizens. This was the sort of decision made by a geriatric oligarchy, and there were plenty of other bad decisions, too. Hove councillors after the war wanted to put a car park under Brunswick Square, a decision which led to the formation of the Regency Society. They aimed to pull down the great Adelaide ramps on the seafront so that the Kingsway could become a dual carriageway, and wereprevented from doing so only by a town poll. They succeeded in demolishing the charming well at St Ann's Well Gardens.

The council was so mean that it neglected the children's playgrounds and had tatty housing, yet it was prepared to spend two and a half million pounds on a new town hall. This was the vision of the one councillor of real ability, a solicitor called Donald Edmonds, who persuaded colleagues to knock down some perfectly serviceable Victorian houses and replace them with a huge ribbed concrete monstrosity *(p.57)*. Grossly out of keeping with its surroundings, the town hall had a clock tower and an atrium which were really wasted space, plus a huge number of public areas, while the office space was so small that the council had to continue using other buildings. It was a remarkable and expensive folly, conceived mainly because Hove had visions of become the centre of a large authority stretching from the Adur to the Ouse. As with nearly every other decision it made, Hove got that one wrong too.

Gradually the council got dragged into the twentieth century, particularly when it merged with Portslade, which meant that all the seats were contested for the first time. Changes to local government also go rid of some dead wood among the officers and brought in men of quality such as Michael Ray, the planning officer, who managed to ensure that not another listed building was lost during his 24-year-reign, which lasted until the amalgamation with Brighton.

There were other events that caused shockwaves too. In 1973, the town's colourless MP Martin Maddan unexpectedly died and there had to be a byelection at the height of the Heath's Government's unpopularity. Politics was a non issue in Hove and the one party even less lively that the Tories was the Liberals, who locally had 'ceased to be' some time in the days of Lloyd George. Yet aided by Des Wilson, a charismatic character who was the director of the housing charity Shelter, they came close to winning the election. Wilson stood again in the first of the 1974 general elections, but by this time Tim Sainsbury, a member of the grocery dynasty, had become well established, and he remained there for another 24 years.

I recall one incident in particular from that byelection. Wilson went to visit a woman on her 100th birthday in Blatchington Road because she was going to vote Liberal. I was invited and arrived early. When I knocked on the door and it was eventually opened by an old crone, I shook her hand warmly and said: 'Congratulations on your 100th birthday.' Just wait a minute,' the old woman replied. 'I'll go and get my mother.'

Tim Sainsbury was like the Brighton councillors in his devotion to public service. As one of Britain's richest men, he need never have lifted a finger, yet he worked mighty hard as a Hove MP and more particularly as a government minister. Solid and unflashy, he was a particular favourite of Michael Heseltine, alleged to like him because no one could then say that Hezza himself was the wealthiest MP. However there was always a slightly remote air about Sainsbury and, because of his enormous wealth, I never quite felt that he knew exactly what it was to be like one of his impoverished elderly customers in the Blatchington Road Sainsbury's.

Opponents criticised Sainsbury for not giving any of his money to the area when he funded the Ashmolean Museum in Oxford and the Sainsbury wing of the National Gallery. But while he was an MP it might have been considered tantamount to bribery. Instead, just after he retired, he quietly made a generous gift to Hove Museum, and that was typical of the man.

Despite its awful council, Hove had and has plenty of interest. Its squares and crescents are among the best in Britain and its Victorian heritage not far behind. It is one of the few towns I know that offers croquet on the lawns, and the only one where you can eat a splendid tea in a fully furnished room of the museum. It has the cricket ground and a dog track, and for many years it was home to Brighton and Hove Albion. Its famous inhabitants have included the man who gave his name to Mount Everest, the great cricketer Sir Jack Hobbs and Patrick Hamilton, who wrote that fine novel *The West Pier*.

Gradually Hove became Brightonised, and a good thing too. Church Road became as much a road of restaurants as Preston Street in Brighton. The lively cosmopolitan atmosphere of Regency ward spilled over into neighbouring Brunswick and the alternative nature of Seven Dials found favour in the nearby Goldsmid area of Hove. The Indian colonels reputed to inhabit Hove faded away, and youngsters started to fill up the flats where pensioners had lived for decades.

It was time for a change and it came with surprising suddenness. Labour, a negligible force in the town, took over the council in 1995 and instituted a lot of changes. Then the merger with Brighton was agreed, so that at last a hundred or more years of history came to an end. Finally, in 1997, Hove elected the council leader, Ivor Caplin, as its first Labour MP. Tony Blair, on hearing the Hove result early the next morning, is said to have remarked: 'Now I *know* I've won!' Hove is just West Brighton these days, and a good thing too.

The Future Which is Yet to Come

*P*eople with little interest in politics who find that for the best part of forty years I have been covering councils often say that it must be boring - and so for a good part of the time it is. There is nothing more mind-numbingly tedious than councillors who come out with phrases like: 'And next I turn to . . .' or: 'And the fourth point I want to make is . . .' But there are some remarkable characters in civic life who have enlivened many a dull day, and they have furnished me with a few stories along the way as well.

There was George Lucraft, not an outstanding character in himself but a man who attracted stories like flypaper . On the day he was made mayor in 1973 there was the usual banquet at the Royal Pavilion. As the throng stood for the loyal toast, a republican socialist called Arthur King (a highly inappropriate name) refused to stand. The outraged and highly patriotic medical officer of health, William

Hove Town Hall, opened in 1974 to replace the previous building destroyed by fire eight years earlier.

Parker, responded by pouring a glass of Yugoslav Riesling (that's what they drank at civic noshes in those days) over his head. Another socialist, Brian Fitch, angrily poured *his* glass over the good doctor's head. It might have gone on in this way until the whole company was sloshed in more than one way had not everyone sat down again to join Councillor King and have a fag.

Only two days later, the Mayor was due to open an archery tournament at Hollingbury in a field facing Carden Avenue. A big burly fellow not used to the sport, the alderman was given the honour of firing the first arrow. It missed the target by miles, soaring upwards and onward for a considerable distance before returning to earth and winging a number 26 bus. These two incidents together afforded George Lucraft more national newspaper publicity in a few days than most mayors get in a lifetime.

Brian Fitch, happily still with us, was a firebrand in those days instead of the elder statesman he is now. With his equally strident colleague, Tom Forester, he accused another Mayor, Alfred Feld, of trying to run them over in the council car park with his white Rolls-Royce. Feld, who had a good sense of humour, managed to make light of the allegations and so won that particular day. He was a flamboyant figure who not only owned the aforesaid Roller but also had an extensive wardrobe, including at least forty suits and a fine selection of ties, some of which he bequeathed to me after hearing that I had a bad tie collection. Al Feld, who started his Brighton life before the war as an impoverished violinist playing nightly at Sherry's in West Street, ended it as a well-loved councillor and joint proprietor, with his equally outlandish wife Lily, of the Norfolk Hotel. They had the philosophy that what was good for the Norfolk must be good for Brighton and good for the Feld family, too, and it worked pretty well.

A more formidable politician was Stanley Theobald, who rose from fairly humble beginnings to become mayor and the most influential councillor of his generation. He had a phenomenal memory and a grasp of detail that served him well both in his chosen career as an estate agent and in his civic rôles. It was reputed that he knew the value of every home in Brighton, and I would not have doubted it. When he spoke in the council chamber he never used a note, even when giving a complicated speech full of financial detail. A short, pugnacious man with a bald pate, Theo (as he was always known) would stand and strut while speaking, an aggressive quality which many people disliked. But he was a formidable foe and a good man to have on your side.

He also got things done. No one before or since has had more council houses built, including the tallest civic tower of all in Blackman Street which now bears his name. His energy was also largely responsible for other great projects, including the building of the Brighton Centre and the creation of the annual arts festival. Though he had many enemies, he was always extraordinarily helpful to me, often pushing titbits of information my way on the most unlikely occasions. His son, Geoffrey, has carried on the family tradition of public service.

Dennis Hobden will always go down in Brighton's history as the first Labour MP in Sussex, and it took another 27 years for any more to join him. Born in Robert Street in 1920, he was like Theo in having a fine memory, and long after old shops had been demolished in what is now the North Laine area he could tell you what was in every one. Through the post office union, Hobden became a great debater and quickly rose through the Labour ranks. He was the ideal man in 1964 to fight the rather languid Tory MP David James, who was more celebrated locally for his quest to find the Loch Ness monster than for helping Brightonians. Aided by students from the newly-created Sussex University, Hobden famously won by seven votes after seven recounts, and so helped Harold Wilson to his victory with a tiny majority.

Concentrating on local issues throughout his six years in Parliament, Hobden quickly became the most celebrated MP of the century in Brighton. Whether it was through his drink-driving case, his divorce or his claim that he could not live on his salary, Hobden was constantly in the headlines. He courted trouble with the Tories for urging closer liaison with the Communists and with his own side for pushing through the Brighton Marina. But he remained relentlessly popular, and when the *Argus* organised an opinion poll 98 per cent of local people had heard of him, then the highest figure ever recorded by any MP.

Defeated at the 1970 election by Andrew Bowden, who eventually became an even more formidable constituency MP, Hobden remained active in politics until his death, even becoming a Labour mayor in what then was still a Tory town. He had some atypical interests for a socialist, being both a mason and a spiritualist. He also loved causing minor mayhem, and had a cheekiness which unusually remained into old age. He was the best mood speaker I ever heard, instantly able to judge an audience, and he was a true fighter for Brighton.

John Smith was the most fearless councillor I ever met. A young Tory with four children, he combined council work with his busy family life and a full time job. He was almost impossible to report for, apart from speaking at 300 words a minute, he would usually take his opponent's argument and ridicule it through ludicrous exaggeration. People would lie helpless with laughter across the leather seats of the council chamber while he spoke.

Once the owner of a seafront club was in the public gallery, waiting to hear the result of some deliberation on the future of his premises. While there, he heard Smith speak in a debate and was so impressed by his comic potential that he challenged the councillor to appear in his club as a 'turn'. Few would have accepted, but Smith did, and - even appearing late at night before a decidedly well lubricated audience - he made them laugh.

Smith was constantly chided by his own side for not being serious enough. Once after I had written a piece about empty phrases, he asked me if I would construct a speech for him composed entirely of clichés. It was easy enough to do, and he uttered it sonorously at a council meeting close to Christmas. Larded with phrases such as 'At this moment in time, I see light at the end of the tunnel and look for the future which is yet to come,' it said precisely nothing for five minutes.

A few of his colleagues got the joke in the end, but many old Tories applauded, and there were not a few cries of: 'Very statesmanlike, John.' Now a management consultant for local government living in Gloucestershire, Smith has moved far away from his former haunts but has appointed a few officers to his old authority. Modestly he claimed to have achieved only two things: banning smoking from the council chamber and renovating Norfolk Square, but he also brought merriment wherever he was, and that is a far greater thing.

Leonard Knowles, the man whose heart was broken when he took over the *Herald*, was also a towering figure in the council chamber. He was a journalist whose coverage of trials at Lewes Assizes he eventually turned into a volume called *Murder in my Notebook*. Len started off as a socialist and, indeed, twice fought the Pavilion seat for Labour at times when it was a hopeless cause. But, wanting to make a political name for himself locally, he joined the Tories and became a formidable operator. Deadly in debate, he entered the fray by perhaps just marking down two words for his notes as bullet points. His dramatic pauses for effect were so long that I was always worried that someone would interrupt them, but no one ever did.

Len had a famous Battle of Sloane Street with Stanley Theobald. He was chairman of planning and wanted the site used for industry while Theo, as housing chairman, wanted flats built there. It was Tory against Tory and the Labour opposition, then pretty small, could only watch and wonder as these political giants slugged it out. Len lost that time, but that was not his finest hour. That came during a debate on comprehensive education. The council was all set to approve this system for the town's schools when Len made a dramatic late intervention in the debate. Before then, most Tories were for the scheme; after it they nearly all voted against. It was a wonderful example to me (even though I didn't agree with the result) of how people can be genuinely swayed by a speech.

When Len answered the phone at his Brighton home with the single word Knowles it echoed down the wires with a fullness that made you realise that you were speaking to someone of substance. It was even more intimidating ringing the town clerk, Bill Dodd. On hearing the one syllable Dodd booming through his amplified handset, many callers misheard it as God. He was popularly known as Almighty Dodd, and a little poem of the time simply ran: 'How odd/Of God/To choose/Bill Dodd.' But he was a great administrator and a fine lawyer. He was a man of total probity, and he was absolutely devoted to Brighton. When he retired it was the end of an era far more than the demise of any single councillor.

It would be wrong to suggest that all the characters were of yesteryear and that our contemporary politicians are a less colourful bunch, but today they are better drilled and less representative of the town. In those days, professional men such as solicitors, lawyers and estate agents wanted to serve Brighton once they had become established in business, so they were already well known before they did so. Now there are hardly any professional men or women on the council, and a goodly proportion of the ruling Labour group are academics. There are dominant figures such as Steve Bassam, the squatter who became a peer and long-time leader of the council, but they don't appear so formidable because the council is much more casually run these days and it's harder to make a mark when debates have become so devalued.

Because the council is so much more open now, important decisions are taken by the political groups, aired in the press and debated many times in committees with the result that by the time they come to the council they are usually tired old issues. There are also only five council meetings a year, whereas they used to be held every four weeks. Long gone are the days when the press bench was full every time and all the local papers sent more than one reporter. Now it's only me, and if I go home after two or three hours through boredom no one from the Fourth Estate is keeping watch on the council at all. I can look at all the names inscribed on the press bench and recall most of them, but I'm not in the least nostalgic. In many ways it's more fun reporting civic life now that it was in the days when formality, pomposity and civic pride burst out of overstrained waistcoats.

A Bald Black Man in a Miniskirt

*B*righton has always been a town for eccentrics and oddities. Nowadays there are so many of them that it's sometimes hard in the centre of town to spot anyone who's entirely normal.

The other day, walking along Gardner Street, I saw a tall, entirely bald, extremely thin, black man wearing nothing but what appeared to be a miniskirt, and no one turned a hair - least of all him! If he'd been in Milton Keynes he'd probably have been arrested. So the reply to people who complain that there are no characters in Brighton any more is that there certainly *are*: it's just that it's hard to stand out against a background of exotic colour.

In those drabber days of the past one man stood out from all his contemporaries and that was Harry Cowley. I would love to have met other characters such as Sir Harry Preston, the bombastic proprietor of the Royal Albion Hotel, and Sir Herbert Carden, the maker of modern Brighton, but I did have the privilege of meeting Cowley. By then he was old and he was past his best, but there was enough fight in the man to make me realise just how formidable he must have been in his prime.

Cowley was an ordinary working man who remained one throughout his long life. He was a chimney sweep born into the sort of grinding poverty that people can hardly imagine now but which was commonplace late last century. He was a natural leader and he had a searing hatred of injustice. Cowley had two trademarks: a bowler hat and a fag permanently stuck to the bottom lip. He also had a catchphrase, 'This don't come right to me', which he used to devastating effect.

After both of the world wars Cowley became angry that homes were not available for all the war heroes, so he made them available himself. Forming a group called the Vigilantes, he took direct action and forced his way into homes which were standing idle. It was hugely effective and it spurred the council to make proper provision for these people. I met him in the late 1960s when the squatting movement was getting under way. Harry was keenly interested and tried to help, but he was too old and the crisis was not quite the same. But he met some of them and the fiery spirit was there.

Cowley was known as the Guv'nor, particularly when he fought for the rights of traders in Upper Gardner Street market. He also campaigned hard for three men he felt had been wrongly convicted of murder to be reprieved, and again he won the day. Nothing was too much trouble for him, and he did it all without any official position or help. He also claimed no honour or reward. But when he died there was one of the biggest funerals Brighton has ever seen at St Peter's Church - and, yes, sure enough, there was a floral bowler.

The then Vicar of Brighton was Canon John Keeling and, amazingly at that time, he was said to have never heard of Cowley, which I felt was typical of the man. Much more interesting was his successor, Canon John Hester, a twinkling, worldly man who'd been Vicar of Soho, a district which he found had much in common with Brighton. He was succeeded by the even more intriguing Canon Dominic Walker, who combined his priestly duties with being one of the top exorcists in the country.

Canon Dominic Walker, the intriguing Vicar of Brighton who later became Bishop of Reading.

Handsome and urbane, Walker had plenty of compassion, too. Once an old man came to me in tears because he was unable to work hard enough for money to pay his poll tax, and he pleaded with me to find him a part time job. I wrote to various notables in the town, MPs, councillors and the rest. The most immediate and effective response came from

Dominic Walker who within a day found the man exactly the job he wanted. It was a fine example of Christianity in action, and many other people knew of kindnesses he had done. There was widespread sorrow in the town when he left to become Bishop of Reading.

From men of God I move to a man regarded by many as the devil incarnate, Nicholas Hoogstraten. When I give talks and mention his name there is always a low frisson of excitement. He must be one of the best known men in town, yet few have ever met him. On the day I arrived in Brighton, Hoogstraten had made the news. Someone had thrown a firebomb through a window and Hoogstraten was alleged to have been implicated. Eventually there was a trial and he was convicted. While in prison he was found guilty of doing nefarious deals with a warden whom he had befriended, and he got his revenge by naming one of his many companies after this man. Hoogstraten was later fined for evicting tenants by chucking their belongings out of the window, declaring: 'That was the best bit of fun I've had for ages.'

Since those wild days when he was a young man Hoogstraten has managed to stay clear of the law and, indeed, now practises his own curious morality. He claims to take action only against tenants he regards as 'scum', and I can report from my own knowledge an elderly tenant who regarded him as a real gent. She wanted nothing more than to stay in the house where she was born at a low rent: Hoogstraten agreed to this, and she stayed there until she had to move into an old folks' home.

Hoogstraten likes to be frightening, which is why he is seldom averse to talking to the press and making provocative statements that might frighten the tenants. He is certainly an imposing man to meet: saturnine, controlled and speaking with a voice that appears to be loaded with menace. On the other hand I have not known him do other than tell the truth. He is also without doubt an expert with money, which is why he appears regularly on the list of the country's richest men.

He started trading in stamps while he was at school, and when he was 21 he was dubbed Britain's youngest millionaire. Soon after that he started his many brushes with the police. At one time he was the biggest private landlord in Brighton and Hove with about

400 properties, not to mention a fair holding in parts of London. But he foresaw the property price collapses in the 1980s, sold most of the houses and put much of his money into gold and antiques. For pleasure he also brought himself a portfolio of hotels, and when seen in Hove he is usually at Courtlands or Langfords.

Hoogstraten is also devoting much time to building a great mansion at Framfield which, when completed, will be one of the largest private homes built in Britain this century. He intends to be buried there, and few will probably see it when he is either alive or dead. His latest battle has been with ramblers who claim that they have a right of way across the estate. This has been comprehensively blocked with a barn and a gate, but the hikers have held a protest there and are determined to win. He may have felt that they were a soft target, and has lived up to his repuation by labelling them scum and riff-raff, but ramblers are a determined bunch, and I would not be at all surprised if they won.

A private man, Hoogstraten remains an enigma, but he is much more complex and interesting than the image of unmitigated evil that he likes to portray.

A man and his mansion. Nicholas Hoogstraten, the Brighton millionaire landlord who likes to keep his tenants in order, is building a palace at Framfield where he will lie in state after death along with his art treasures.

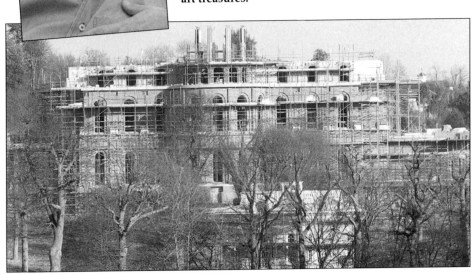

One of my favourite characters was Julian Amery, the MP for Brighton Pavilion between 1969 and 1992. He was often criticised for not attending more to his constituency, but he came from an era when you went there a few times a year and were praised for doing so. His father, Leo, was a Cabinet Minister, and young Julian spent his childhood in their wonderful house at Eaton Square in Belgravia, meeting many of the leading politicians of the day.

He had a remarkable war, performing brave acts in countries such as Albania and Yugoslavia before coming back and entering the political fray. He became MP for Preston and married Catherine, daughter of the Prime Minister, Harold Macmillan. In an act of nepotism 'Supermac' appointed him to the government, where he became minister of aviation.

Amery lost his seat at Preston in 1966, and the following year was selected for Brighton Pavilion, The Conservatives felt that they were choosing a statesman, possibly a future foreign secretary. In that they were to be sorely disappointed. Amery held various positions in the Heath administration but never high office, while Margaret Thatcher passed him over completely despite sharing many of his views. Although elected in a byelection on his 50th birthday, Amery already appeared old, with his ponderous gait and deliberate manner of speaking. He also had a fondness for drink, which may have prevented his promotion.

But he was wonderful company, particularly over lunch. He had known everyone, and was able to talk about these people completely without rancour or malice. The lunches would last a long time and much drink would be consumed. Amery would then enter an unofficial competition for the shortest taxi ride in Brighton to reach his next appointment: once I recall him taking a cab from the foot of West Street to the Royal Albion Hotel.

I never saw him the worse for drink, although he had a method of standing with his legs far apart which prevented him from falling over. On election nights in the Dome, he would make an inaudible speech while assorted Trots in the audience foamed and threw things at him. Although not in Brighton a great deal, he had a house in Sussex near his father in law's mansion and had wonderful connections. If a constituent wrote to him with a problem, he knew exactly where to go for the answer. He never lost his zest for travel, and even in old age would endure privations in faraway places to meet old friends.

When he died there was a memorial service at St Margaret's, Westminster, attended by the great and the good but also by a few unconventionally dressed people, many from foreign lands, whom he had befriended over the years. At the service Winston Churchill MP gave a quote I had not heard before but which summed up the man. It was: 'Between the revolution and the firing squad there is always time for a bottle of champagne.'

His opponent in the 1969 byelection for Labour was Tom Skeffington-Lodge, a tall man with a booming voice who had been Labour MP for Bedford after the war. Skeff was 64 at the time, and it is inconceivable that the party would have chosen someone like him today. He invited Tony Benn, then technology minster, to speak for him at Stanford School, but the meeting was so poorly advertised that only six people turned up. Abandoning his prepared speech, Benn took us on a wonderfully enthusiastic ramble through technology, drawing all over the blackboard. I wonder what the children made of it next day.

Skeff stayed in Brighton for more than twenty years until his death, and he entertained royally at his fine home in Powis Grove - so much so that most of the leading Labour lights of the day came to stay there. A confirmed bachelor, Skeff was the butt of scurrilous stories in *Private Eye* which always delighted in using his name as an address. But he was wonderfully entertaining and remained true to his Christian Socialist principles until the end.

Also a toff, although he would never have admitted it, was Bruno Crosby, leader of the squatters in Brighton during the 1970s. Long haired and scruffy, Bruno looked the part but he was rumoured to come from posh stock and have a doting, aristocratic mother. Whether this was true I never found out, but what was undoubtedly true was that almost everyone liked him. He was a gentle, endearing, unworldly fellow with a hesitant manner and a lisp.

Eventually, with some friends, he found an empty house near Preston Circus where, much to their surprise, the landlords did not take their usual court action and boot them out. Instead Bruno and company made the place into a proper home. They even joined the local residents' association and the council leader of the time, Bob

Cristofoli, once went round there for tea. They might be there today had they been able to claim the squatters' rights which they could have done after seven years. But, much to Bruno's chagrin, the landlord mysteriously reappeared from deepest Dorset just a couple of days before the time span was over, and poor old Bruno had to move. Soon after that he left Brighton and was never heard of again. I like to think that he is still amiably squatting somewhere else, but he's probably highly respectable and married with two kids living in a mansion.

Another squatter was Steve Bassam, one of the most dominant figures in today's Brighton. I first met him more than twenty years ago in a squat on the seafront in Kemp Town, looking vaguely like John Lennon. Even then he showed his tenacity and leadership qualities, supplanting Bruno as the squatters' spokesman. He went to Sussex University and, like so many other graduates, decided to stay in Brighton. The town has been a graveyard of many ambitions, but not for Steve Bassam. He quickly found himself on Brighton Council, and I remember him literally leaping in the air with joy when the election result was declared at the Dome.

The squatter who became a peer: Lord 'Steve' Bassam, leader ofBrighton and Hove Council.

Within no time at all he was deputy leader of the Labour opposition group, and he remained so when his party gained control of the council in 1986. Within another couple of years he'd become leader, and three years later he erased the rule that no one should lead the council for more than that period. He took a big gamble on betting that Brighton and Hove would become a unitary council and that labour would win the election. Then he became leader of the new authority.

Now nationally known, Bassam still surprised many people, including me, when he was appointed a peer in 1997 by Tony Blair.

Many pictures were shown of him in his squatting days, including the time he wore a flashing red nose in court before an unamused county court judge. There was also some comparison between his old temporary homes and the rather fine building he bought at auction in Kemp Town and where he now lives.

What is remarkable about Lord Bassam is how, without apparent bossiness, he became the natural leader of Labour in Brighton, and how he swung them into power by moderating their position. He was a Blairite before Tony Blair was invented. He also has an immense capacity for hard work, often rising in the small hours to dictate letters. He has a full time job, goes to the Lords, leads the council and has a family life. I don't know how he fits it all in, and I suspect that, just occasionally, he doesn't.

Bassam doesn't always win his battles. He failed to defeat Sir Andrew Bowden in Kemp Town in 1987 and he never succeeded in getting a supermarket and park-and-ride scheme at Patcham. But he is prepared to be bold and take risks, an attractive quality in a politician, and - irrespective of politics - he, like most of the other people mentioned in this book, really does love Brighton.

Secret Places

When people think of Brighton, they have an image of the seafront and the town centre, but I like many other parts of the place that few visit or appreciate. That's partly because I have made it my business to know Brighton pretty well: I know most streets in the town and, for that matter, most of those in Hove, Portslade, Southwick and Shoreham, too.

At least once every year I venture into the far flung places just to keep in touch. Not many others do this, for unless you live in one of the suburbs, have friends there or work as a taxi driver there is no particular reason for visiting them. This is why many who have lived all their lives in the area have never once been to places such as Bevendean or Mile Oak, stuck as they are a mile or two up valleys which are cul de sacs - at least if you are travelling by road.

They are missing a thing or two.

Mile Oak, known as Nappy Valley in the 1960s because of the cheap housing which was snapped up by young families, has an unlovely layout which is confusing to the stranger. Yet it is redeemed by the surrounding countryside, especially by Southwick Hill. The

Southwick Hill, one of the secret delights of Sussex, with the less lovely Mile Oak and Foredown Hill.

Society of Sussex Downsmen initially wondered whether to bother opposing the Brighton bypass, thinking that the downland might be too urbanised and scraggy to be worth preserving. But after visiting Southwick Hill with its fine, natural turf, they changed their minds. There's a wonderful network of footpaths leading from the hill, and local people gain such evident pleasure from being there.

Just below it is Portslade Old Village, more ancient than any part of Hove, and far prettier. There are still narrow streets with flint walls and an unexpected field used for rescuing horses fallen on bad times. Best of all is the Emmaus Centre for the homeless, a former convent. The buildings are not particularly special, but the wondrful gardens are linked by a tunnel under the road. Another survivor is the Foredown Tower, an old water tower now housing a *camera obscura* through which you can spy on the surrounding countryside.

Nearby is Benfield Valley, saved from development by the building of a Sainsbury's store in just one part of it. That was part of the planning gain offered to Hove by Sainsbury's, and I always suspected that Sir Tim had something to do with it. Despite the store, the link road and the bypass, there is still a lot of wildlife left, especially on Benfield Hill where, if you are lucky, you can spot deer, badgers and even glow worms.

Hangleton is now mainly suburbia, but the old Dyke Railway has been converted into a pleasant bridleway with a predictably gentle gradient. It is a shame that the line closed when it did, because now it would be an enormous tourist attraction. Hangleton Manor is the oldest secular building in Hove. Now a pub, it is worth visiting, not only for the beer, but for the Ten Commandments painted on one of the ceilings and for a restored dovecote in the grounds.

Three Cornered Copse is a pleasant swathe of countryside leading right from the Downs to meet a corner of Hove Park. You can walk on green nearly all the way from the top of Dyke Road right down to the Old Shoreham Road. As you do so you can catch a glimpse of the British Engineerium, an old pumping station wonderfully restored by Jonathan Minns, one of those enthusiasts who makes things happen. Hangleton's best secret is The Hyde, a club occupying the old Alliance and Leicester sports club near the Grenadier. Partly owned by the boxer Chris Eubank, it is a pleasant place to visit and still has its own sports field.

A few hundred yards south of that is Hove Cemetery, a cul de sac in more ways than one. There's plenty of wildlife, including a fox which you can often see from the Coastway West railway line, and a few well known people are buried there, notably Sir Jack Hobbs, the great Surrey and England batsmen, who made his home in Hove. Tucked behind Portland Road is Davis Park, until recently a rose garden but now just a pleasant oasis of greenery known to only those who live nearby.

Westdene can boast Coney Hill, a surprising stretch of coun-tryside broken only by vent holes for the London to Brighton railway line as it passes through a tunnel. The chief building nearby is Patcham Mill, privately owned but occasionally open to the public. One of the last mills to be built in Sussex, it commands views of the Isle of Wight. When I first came to Brighton, it was on sale for just £5,000, only £1,000 more than the modest terraced house I found. I knew it was a huge bargain and wished that I could have bought it, and it's now worth more than several terraced houses put together.

Some pleasant and surprisingly extensive woodland exists in Westdene and in neighbouring Withdean. It survived because it was extremely hilly or because it was near the railway line, and it lends a sylvan air to this part of suburbia. Patcham has a pleasing old village with another decent (and listed) dovecote and a row of fine old cottages up Church Hill. The Chattri memorial to Indian soldiers who died in the First World War is on the downs about half a mile north - a fine place from which to contemplate the futility of fighting.

Hollingbury Hillfort is one of the highest points in Brighton, with wonderful sweeping views. Nearby is the Wild Park, still aptly named, and there are more woods dipping down towards the Roedale allotments. Behind Bevendean there are some fine country walks: when in the valleys you would never think that you were anywhere near Brighton. Even more remote is Castle Hill, a Site of Special Scientific Interest about a mile east of Woodingdean, and it was there that I once gained some of my best ever views of badgers. Drove Road, an ancient track which runs parallel to Warren Road, gives rather fine views across the Bevendean Valley. Near the end you can view the house in McWilliam Road once occupied briefly and incongruously by Errol Flynn. It was bought later by the Labour MP Dennis Hobden, who revelled in its quirky associations.

Ovingdean village is an unappreciated part of Brighton, with a few fine houses and an ancient church just as good as any over the hill in Rottingdean. And one of the great glories of Brighton is Roedean School. It is open suprisingly often for concerts and other performances, mainly in the splendid theatre which is as big as the Gardner Centre at Sussex University. Started rather over a century ago, Roedean's building dates mainly from then, but additions have been made in practically every decade to form a fascinating and odd medley of styles.

The sewers in Brighton have been made into a tourist attraction by the Brighton Festival. Now author and guide Maire

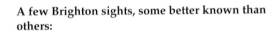

A few Brighton sights, some better known than others:

The town's famous Victorian sewers (*left*) are open for guided tours during the arts festival each May. Designed by Sir John Hawkshaw, and begun in 1871, they're still in use today.

Roedean (*below*), probably the best known girls' public school in Britain, has a magnificent setting on the Downs just east of Brighton.

McQueeney has done much the same for the great gaunt cemeteries off Lewes Road. They are even more full of wildlife than the Hove ones, and the tombs are that much more ornate. The great engine builder Herbert Stroudley is buried here together with a host of other eminent Victorians and a veritable chain of mayors. Towering above them is Brighton General Hospital, whose fine Italian façade I hope will remain even if it is converted into housing, and behind that is Brighton Racecourse, seedy and somewhat decrepit but reeking of two hundred years of sporting history. On a fine day the sight of the horses speeding towards you from the back of Woodingdean is still stirring.

Ornate tombstones *(right)* amid the Gothic grandeur of the cemeteries off Lewes Road remember many of the town's great and good.

Brighton General Hospital *(below)*, high on a hill with the racecourse just behind it, was originally the Elm Grove workhouse.

Of course I love the great terraces and squares of Regency Brighton, but my favourite street of all is far less well known. It is Montpelier Villas, short but almost perfectly formed. Some of the smaller squares like Powis, Russell and Bedford still have a period charm while Montpelier Crescent and Park Crescent have two of the best unappreciated sweeps in the town. For an example of early town planning, look at the Roundhill area from the Race Hill and see how fine it is .

Brighton is known for its twittens, one of the few words of genuine Sussex dialect to have survived. Those round the Lanes are finest, but I confess a liking for Boundary Passage which, as its name suggests, marks the divide with Hove. There are quiet places even in the heart of town, among them the gardens of St Nicholas Church to the west of Dyke Road, where you can sit alone most days while thousands throng Churchill Square just two hundred yards away.

I love the great Victorian churches of Brighton. St Peter's, designed by Charles Barry (who also built the Royal Sussex County Hospital before moving on to the Houses of Parliament) is best, and is really the cathedral of the town. But St Bartholomew's, the highest church in England, must run it close, and more can appreciate its imposing interior now that it is open daily to the public. St Martin's off Lewes Road and St Michael's in Victoria Road are two under-appreciated, although enormous, churches while St Paul's in West Street, the fishermen's church, has been impeccably restored.

St George's in Kemp Town will be much more visited once the crypt, which includes an impressive memorial to the Peel family, is opened to the public. I also like All Saints in Hove, another fine church undergoing restoration. Another well worth visiting is the Church of the Annunciation, hidden away among terraced housing in Washington Street, an unlikely setting for windows designed by Burne-Jones. Holy Trinity, now an art gallery in Ship Street, is really a shrine to the wonderful preacher and social reformer Frederick Robertson. St Patrick's in Cambridge Road is testimony to the ongoing work for the homeless by Father Alan Sharpe and his son Stephen. I wish a use could be found for nearby St Andrew's, another work by Barry, which is astoundingly beautiful inside.

Brighton is really a city by the sea, although not yet in name, but you are never far from the Downs surrounding it. Even in Bond

Street, right in the heart of town, you can suddenly catch a glimpse of Hollingbury Downs; while, looking down Addison Road off Dyke Road, you have a clear view of the Downs rolling to the west. And you are never far from greenery in town either. Dyke Road Park, opposite the Booth Museum, is one of my favourite places. Pelham Square off Trafalgar Street would be splendid if only they could find some way of removing the drunks.

Brighton is really a big collection of villages and they are changing all the time. During my comparatively short period here North Laine has become amazingly bohemian and trendy, West Hill arty and Hanover hip. Florence Road has become an enclave for the universities and Seven Dials has become a real 24-hour part of town. By contrast, Montpelier has become much less posh, losing its larger than life characters such as the playwright Alan Melville and broadcaster Gilbert Harding, while Kemp Town has slowly become sleazier.

There's an amazingly hard light in Brighton, especially near the sea, possibly because of the absence of vegetation. It shows up every crack and wrinkle on the old girl's facade, but it also makes the town appear endlessly fascinating as it illuminates all the odd corners I have mentioned.

The Brighton Buzz

*I*nevitably books of this nature tend to dwell in the past. But I once heard Lord Brockway speak at the Brighton Centre when he was well over ninety, and he looked only to the future. Brighton has had an enviably exciting history, but I firmly believe that the best is yet to come. Indeed, there was a certain amount of stagnation during most of the years I was in Brighton, which has only recently been superseded by what people like to term the Brighton Buzz.

The town has been fortunate in not being ruined by urban motorways or by huge swathes of unsuitable buildings. Mistakes were made, notably in the 1960s when many fine buildings were lost and many awful ones erected in their place. But Brighton has an enviable heritage and it is unlikely that many, if any, of its listed buildings will be lost in the future.

Restoration of the Old Market in Hove has been completed, and the West Pier should be ready early next century. The Brunswick and Kemp Town seafronts are looking the best they have done for years. And the Lower Promenade between the piers is full of life after being tatty for decades.

Brighton seems to have come to a balance with its transport, despite its huge influx of people and narrow streets. It is one of the few provincial towns with a decent bus service. Plenty of people use their feet and bikes to get about, and traffic jams are not as bad as elsewhere. There's a lot of high tech industry moving into the town to replace the old engineering firms, and the town is also a big financial centre. But most of all it is a tourist town and revels in being outrageous. It is a town where people can have fun at almost any time, and it is especially attractive to youngsters. That in turn gives it a zest and vitality which few, if any, other seaside resorts in Britain possess.

Many companies seem willing to invest in Brighton's future, particularly in the leisure and entertainment industries. At the same time, money from the Lottery and the Government is being used both to transform the deprived sections of town and to renovate glories such as the Dome and the museum. Fine new buildings such as a central library are planned, and £18 million has been spent on the railway station. It's an exciting place to be at this time.

I hope to remain faithfully recording the constantly changing scene for a few more years yet, watching Brighton move purposefully into the Millennium. Brighton will remain infuriating, argumentative, awkward and frustrating, but it is a matchless place to write about and I have been lucky to have been given that chance.

Adam Trimingham
May, 1999

INDEX